Boston Red Sox 2021

A Baseball Companion

Edited by Steven Goldman and Bret Sayre

Baseball Prospectus

Craig Brown, Associate Editor
Robert Au, Harry Pavlidis and Amy Pircher, Statistics Editors

Copyright © 2021 by DIY Baseball, LLC.
All rights reserved

This book or any part thereof may not be reproduced or transmitted in any form or by any means, electronic or mechanical, including photocopying, recording, or by any information storage and retrieval system, without permission in writing from the publisher.

Limit of Liability/Disclaimer of Warranty: While the publisher and the author have used their best efforts in preparing this book, they make no representations or warranties with respect to the accuracy or completeness of the contents of this book and specifically disclaim any implied warranties of merchantability or fitness for a particular purpose. No warranty may be created or extended by sales representatives or written sales materials. The advice and strategies contained herein may not be suitable for your situation. You should consult with a professional where appropriate. Neither the publisher nor the author shall be liable for any loss of profit or any other commercial damages, including but not limited to special, incidental, consequential, or other damages.

Library of Congress Cataloging-in-Publication Data:
paperback
ISBN-13: 978-1-950716-31-9

Project Credits
Cover Design: Ginny Searle
Interior Design and Production: Amy Pircher, Robert Au
Layout: Amy Pircher, Robert Au

Baseball icon courtesy of Uberux, from https://www.shareicon.net/author/uberux

Ballpark diagram courtesy of Lou Spirito/THIRTY81 Project, https://thirty81project.com/

Manufactured in the United States of America
10 9 8 7 6 5 4 3 2 1

Table of Contents

Statistical Introduction v

Part 1: Team Analysis

Performance Graphs 3
2020 Team Performance 4
2021 Team Projections 5
Team Personnel 6
Fenway Park Stats 7
Red Sox Team Analysis 9

Part 2: Player Analysis

Red Sox Player Analysis 16
Red Sox Prospects 103

Part 3: Featured Articles

Red Sox All-Time Top 10 Players 117
    by Rob Mains

A Taxonomy of 2020 Abnormalities 123
    by Rob Mains

Tranches of WAR 129
    by Russell A. Carleton

Secondhand Sport 135
    by Patrick Dubuque

Steve Dalkowski Dreaming 139
    by Steven Goldman

A Reward For A Functioning Society 143
    by Cory Frontin and Craig Goldstein

Index of Names 147

Statistical Introduction

Sports are, fundamentally, a blend of athletic endeavor and storytelling. Baseball, like any other sport, tells its stories in so many ways: in the arc of a game from the stands or a season from the box scores, in photos, or even in numbers. At Baseball Prospectus, we understand that statistics don't replace observation or any of baseball's stories, but complement everything else that makes the game so much fun.

What stats help us with is with patterns and precision, variance and value. This book can help you learn things you may not see from watching a game or hundred, whether it's the path of a career over time or the breadth of the entire MLB. We'd also never ask you to choose between our numbers and the experience of viewing a game from the cheap seats or the comfort of your home; our publication combines running the numbers with observations and wisdom from some of the brightest minds we can find. But if you *do* want to learn more about the numbers beyond what's on the backs of player jerseys, let us help explain.

Offense

We've revised our methodology for determining batting value. Long-time readers of the book will notice that we've retired True Average in favor of a new metric: Deserved Runs Created Plus (DRC+). Developed by Jonathan Judge and our stats team, this statistic measures everything a player does at the plate–reaching base, hitting for power, making outs, and moving runners over–and puts it on a scale where 100 equals league-average performance. A DRC+ of 150 is terrific, a DRC+ of 100 is average and a DRC+ of 75 means you better be an excellent defender.

DRC+ also does a better job than any of our previous metrics in taking contextual factors into account. The model adjusts for how the park affects performance, but also for things like the talent of the opposing pitcher, value of different types of batted-ball events, league, temperature and other factors. It's able to describe a player's expected offensive contribution than any other statistic we've found over the years, and also does a better job of predicting future performance as well.

The other aspect of run-scoring is baserunning, which we quantify using Baserunning Runs. BRR not only records the value of stolen bases (or getting caught in the act), but also accounts for all the stuff that doesn't show up on the back of a baseball card: a runner's ability to go first to third on a single, or advance on a fly ball.

Defense

Where offensive value is *relatively* easy to identify and understand, defensive value is … not. Over the past dozen years, the sabermetric community has focused mostly on stats based on zone data: a real-live human person records the type of batted ball and estimated landing location, and models are created that give expected outs. From there, you can compare fielders' actual outs to those expected ones. Simple, right?

Unfortunately, zone data has two major issues. First, zone data is recorded by commercial data providers who keep the raw data private unless you pay for it. (All the statistics we build in this book and on our website use public data as inputs.) That hurts our ability to test assumptions or duplicate results. Second, over the years it has become apparent that there's quite a bit of "noise" in zone-based fielding analysis. Sometimes the conclusions drawn from zone data don't hold up to scrutiny, and sometimes the different data provided by different providers don't look anything alike, giving wildly different results. Sometimes the hard-working professional stringers or scorers might unknowingly inflict unconscious bias into the mix: for example good fielders will often be credited with more expected outs despite the data, and ballparks with high press boxes tend to score more line drives than ones with a lower press box.

Enter our Fielding Runs Above Average (FRAA). For most positions, FRAA is built from play-by-play data, which allows us to avoid the subjectivity found in many other fielding metrics. The idea is this: count how many fielding plays are made by a given player and compare that to expected plays for an average fielder at their position (based on pitcher ground ball tendencies and batter handedness). Then we adjust for park and base-out situations.

When it comes to catchers, our methodology is a little different thanks to the laundry list of responsibilities they're tasked with beyond just, well, catching and throwing the ball. By now you've probably heard about "framing" or the art of making umpires more likely to call balls outside the strike zone for strikes. To put this into one tidy number, we incorporate pitch tracking data (for the years it exists) and adjust for important factors like pitcher, umpire, batter and home-field advantage using a mixed-model approach. This grants us a number for how many strikes the catcher is personally adding to (or subtracting from) his pitchers' performance … which we then convert to runs added or lost using linear weights.

Framing is one of the biggest parts of determining catcher value, but we also take into account blocking balls from going past, whether a scorer deems it a passed ball or a wild pitch. We use a similar approach—one that really benefits from the pitch tracking data that tells us what ends up in the dirt and what doesn't. We also include a catcher's ability to prevent stolen bases and how well they field balls in play, and *finally* we come up with our FRAA for catchers.

Pitching

Both pitching and fielding make up the half of baseball that isn't run scoring: run prevention. Separating pitching from fielding is a tough task, and most recent pitching analysis has branched off from Voros McCracken's famous (and controversial) statement, "There is little if any difference among major-league pitchers in their ability to prevent hits on balls hit in the field of play." The research of the analytic community has validated this to some extent, and there are a host of "defense-independent" pitching measures that have been developed to try and extract the effect of the defense behind a hurler from the pitcher's work.

Our solution to this quandary is Deserved Run Average (DRA), our core pitching metric. DRA seeks to evaluate a pitcher's performance, much like earned run average (ERA), the tried-and-true pitching stat you've seen on every baseball broadcast or box score from the past century, but it's very different. To start, DRA takes an event-by-event look at what the pitchers does, and adjusts the value of that event based on different environmental factors like park, batter, catcher, umpire, base-out situation, run differential, inning, defense, home field advantage, pitcher role and temperature. That mixed model gives us a pitcher's expected contribution, similar to what we do for our DRC+ model for hitters and FRAA model for catchers. (Oh, and we also consider the pitcher's effect on basestealing and on balls getting past the catcher.)

DRA is set to the scale of runs allowed per nine innings (RA9) instead of ERA, which makes DRA's scale slightly higher than ERA's. Because of this, for ease of use, we're supplying DRA-, which is much easier for the reader to parse. As with DRC+, DRA- is an "index" stat, meaning instead of using some arbitrary and shifting number to denote what's "good," average is always 100. The reason that it uses a minus rather than a plus is because like ERA, a lower number is better. Therefore a 75 DRA- describes a performance 25 percent better than average, whereas a 150 DRA- means that either a pitcher is getting extremely lucky with their results, or getting ready to try a new pitch.

Since the last time you picked up an edition of this book, we've also made a few minor changes to DRA to make it better. Recent research into "tunneling"—the act of throwing consecutive pitches that appear similar from a batter's point of view until after the swing decision point–data has given us a new contextual factor to account for in DRA: plate distance. This refers to the distance between successive pitches as they approach the plate, and while it has a smaller effect than factors like velocity or whiff rate, it still can help explain pitcher strikeout rate in our model.

Recently Added Descriptive Statistics

Returning to our 2021 edition of the book are a few figures which recently appeared. These numbers may be a little bit more familiar to those of you who have spent some time investigating baseball statistics.

Fastball Percentage

Our fastball percentage (FA%) statistic measures how frequently a pitcher throws a pitch classified as a "fastball," measured as a percentage of overall pitches thrown. We qualify three types of fastballs:

1. The traditional four-seam fastball;
2. The two-seam fastball or sinker;
3. "Hard cutters," which are pitches that have the movement profile of a cut fastball and are used as the pitcher's primary offering or in place of a more traditional fastball.

For example, a pitcher with a FA% of 67 throws any combination of these three pitches about two-thirds of the time.

Whiff Rate

Everybody loves a swing and a miss, and whiff rate (Whiff%) measures how frequently pitchers induce a swinging strike. To calculate Whiff%, we add up all the pitches thrown that ended with a swinging strike, then divide that number by a pitcher's total pitches thrown. Most often, high whiff rates correlate with high strikeout rates (and overall effective pitcher performance).

Called Strike Probability

Called Strike Probability (CSP) is a number that represents the likelihood that all of a pitcher's pitches will be called a strike while controlling for location, pitcher and batter handedness, umpire and count. Here's how it works: on each pitch, our model determines how many times (out of 100) that a similar pitch was called for a strike given those factors mentioned above, and when normalized for each batter's strike zone. Then we average the CSP for all pitches thrown by a pitcher in a season, and that gives us the yearly CSP percentage you see in the stats boxes.

As you might imagine, pitchers with a higher CSP are more likely to work in the zone, where pitchers with a lower CSP are likely locating their pitches outside the normal strike zone, for better or for worse.

Projections

Many of you aren't turning to this book just for a look at what a player has done, but for a look at what a player is going to do: the PECOTA projections. PECOTA, initially developed by Nate Silver (who has moved on to greater fame as a political analyst), consists of three parts:

1. Major-league equivalencies, which use minor-league statistics to project how a player will perform in the major leagues;
2. Baseline forecasts, which use weighted averages and regression to the mean to estimate a player's current true talent level; and
3. Aging curves, which uses the career paths of comparable players to estimate how a player's statistics are likely to change over time.

With all those important things covered, let's take a look at what's in the book this year.

Team Prospectus

Most of this book is composed of team chapters, with one for each of the 30 major-league franchises. On the first page of each chapter, you'll see a box that contains some of the key statistics for each team as well as a very inviting stadium diagram.

We start with the team name, their unadjusted 2020 win-loss record, and their divisional ranking. Beneath that are a host of other team statistics. **Pythag** presents an adjusted 2020 winning percentage, calculated by taking runs scored per game (**RS/G**) and runs allowed per game (**RA/G**) for the team, and running them through a version of Bill James' Pythagorean formula that was refined and improved by David Smyth and Brandon Heipp. (The formula is called "Pythagenpat," which is equally fun to type and to say.)

Next up is **DRC+**, described earlier, to indicate the overall hitting ability of the team either above or below league-average. Run prevention on the pitching side is covered by **DRA** (also mentioned earlier) and another metric: Fielding Independent Pitching (**FIP**), which calculates another ERA-like statistic based on strikeouts, walks, and home runs recorded. Defensive Efficiency Rating (**DER**) tells us the percentage of balls in play turned into outs for the team, and is a quick fielding shorthand that rounds out run prevention.

After that, we have several measures related to roster composition, as opposed to on-field performance. **B-Age** and **P-Age** tell us the average age of a team's batters and pitchers, respectively. **Payroll** is the combined team payroll for all on-field players, and Doug Pappas' Marginal Dollars per Marginal Win (**M$/MW**) tells us how much money a team spent to earn production above replacement level.

Next to each of these stats, we've listed each team's MLB rank in that category from first to 30th. In this, first always indicates a positive outcome and 30th a negative outcome, except in the case of salary—first is highest.

After the franchise statistics, we share a few items about the team's home ballpark. There's the aforementioned diagram of the park's dimensions (including distances to the outfield wall), a graphic showing the height of the wall from the left-field pole to the right-field pole, and a table showing three-year park factors for the stadium. The park factors are displayed as indexes where 100 is average, 110 means that the park inflates the statistic in question by 10 percent, and 90 means that the park deflates the statistic in question by 10 percent.

On the second page of each team chapter, you'll find three graphs. The first is **Payroll History** and helps you see how the team's payroll has compared to the MLB and divisional average payrolls over time. Payroll figures are current as of January 1, 2021; with so many free agents still unsigned as of this writing, the final 2021 figure will likely be significantly different for many teams. (In the meantime, you can always find the most current data at Baseball Prospectus' Cot's Baseball Contracts page.)

The second graph is **Future Commitments** and helps you see the team's future outlays, if any.

The third graph is **Farm System Ranking** and displays how the Baseball Prospectus prospect team has ranked the organization's farm system since 2007.

After the graphs, we have a **Personnel** section that lists many of the important decision-makers and upper-level field and operations staff members for the franchise, as well as any former Baseball Prospectus staff members who are currently part of the organization. (In very rare circumstances, someone might be on both lists!)

Position Players

After all that information and a thoughtful bylined essay covering each team, we present our player comments. These are also bylined, but due to frequent franchise shifts during the offseason, our bylines are more a rough guide than a perfect accounting of who wrote what.

Each player is listed with the major-league team that employed him as of early January 2021. If a player changed teams after that point via free agency, trade, or any other method, you'll be able to find them in the chapter for their previous squad.

As an example, take a look at the player comment for Padres shortstop Fernando Tatis Jr.: the stat block that accompanies his written comment is at the top of this page. First we cover biographical information (age is as of June 30, 2021) before moving onto the stats themselves. Our statistic columns include standard identifying information like **YEAR**, **TEAM**, **LVL** (level of affiliated play) and **AGE** before getting into the numbers. Next, we provide raw, untranslated

Fernando Tatis Jr. SS
Born: 01/02/99 Age: 22 Bats: R Throws: R
Height: 6'3" Weight: 217 Origin: International Free Agent, 2015

YEAR	TEAM	LVL	AGE	PA	R	2B	3B	HR	RBI	BB	K	SB	CS	AVG/OBP/SLG
2018	SA	AA	19	394	77	22	4	16	43	33	109	16	5	.286/.355/.507
2019	SD	MLB	20	372	61	13	6	22	53	30	110	16	6	.317/.379/.590
2020	SD	MLB	21	257	50	11	2	17	45	27	61	11	3	.277/.366/.571
2021 FS	SD	MLB	22	600	95	24	4	31	81	50	165	17	8	.263/.331/.499
2021 DC	SD	MLB	22	628	100	25	4	32	85	53	173	19	8	.263/.331/.499

Comparables: Darryl Strawberry, Bo Bichette, Ronald Acuña Jr.

YEAR	TEAM	LVL	AGE	PA	DRC+	BABIP	BRR	FRAA	WARP
2018	SA	AA	19	394	136	.370	3.0	SS(83): -1.9	2.4
2019	SD	MLB	20	372	118	.410	7.1	SS(83): 0.9	3.4
2020	SD	MLB	21	257	126	.306	0.7	SS(57): -5.5	0.9
2021 FS	SD	MLB	22	600	126	.318	1.7	SS -1	3.9
2021 DC	SD	MLB	22	628	126	.318	1.8	SS -1	4.0

numbers like you might find on the back of your dad's baseball cards: **PA** (plate appearances), **R** (runs), **2B** (doubles), **3B** (triples), **HR** (home runs), **RBI** (runs batted in), **BB** (walks), **K** (strikeouts), **SB** (stolen bases) and **CS** (caught stealing).

Following the basic stats is **Whiff%** (whiff rate), which denotes how often, when a batter swings, he fails to make contact with the ball. Another way to think of this number is an inverse of a hitter's contact rate.

Next, we have unadjusted "slash" statistics: **AVG** (batting average), **OBP** (on-base percentage) and **SLG** (slugging percentage). Following the slash line is **DRC+** (Deserved Runs Created Plus), which we described earlier as total offensive expected contribution compared to the league average.

BABIP (batting average on balls in play) tells us how often a ball in play fell for a hit, and can help us identify whether a batter may have been lucky or not ... but note that high BABIPs also tend to follow the great hitters of our time, as well as speedy singles hitters who put the ball on the ground.

The next item is **BRR** (Baserunning Runs), which covers all of a player's baserunning accomplishments including (but not limited to) swiped bags and failed attempts. Next is **FRAA** (Fielding Runs Above Average), which also includes the number of games previously played at each position noted in parentheses. Multi-position players have only their two most frequent positions listed here, but their total FRAA number reflects all positions played.

Our last column here is **WARP** (Wins Above Replacement Player). WARP estimates the total value of a player, which means for hitters it takes into account hitting runs above average (calculated using the DRC+ model), BRR and FRAA. Then, it makes an adjustment for positions played and gives the player a credit for plate appearances based upon the difference between "replacement level"—which is derived from the quality of players added to a team's roster after the start of the season—and the league average.

The final line just below the stats box is **PECOTA** data, which is discussed further in a following section.

Catchers

Catchers are a special breed, and thus they have earned their own separate box which displays some of the defensive metrics that we've built just for them. As an example, let's check out Yasmani Grandal.

YEAR	TEAM	P. COUNT	FRM RUNS	BLK RUNS	THRW RUNS	TOT RUNS
2018	LAD	16816	15.7	0.8	0.1	16.5
2019	MIL	18740	19.4	1.8	-0.1	21.1
2020	CHW	4830	3.7	0.3	-0.2	3.8
2021	CHW	14430	16.7	-0.6	1.0	17.1
2021	CHW	14430	16.7	0.4	1.0	18.0

The **YEAR** and **TEAM** columns match what you'd find in the other stat box. **P. COUNT** indicates the number of pitches thrown while the catcher was behind the plate, including swinging strikes, fouls and balls in play. **FRM RUNS** is the total run value the catcher provided (or cost) his team by influencing the umpire to call strikes where other catchers did not. **BLK RUNS** expresses the total run value above or below average for the catcher's ability to prevent wild pitches and passed balls. **THRW RUNS** is calculated using a similar model as the previous two statistics, and it measures a catcher's ability to throw out basestealers but also to dissuade them from testing his arm in the first place. It takes into account factors like the pitcher (including his delivery and pickoff move) and baserunner (who could be as fast as Billy Hamilton or as slow as Yonder Alonso). **TOT RUNS** is the sum of all of the previous three statistics.

Pitchers

Let's give our pitchers a turn, using 2020 AL Cy Young winner Shane Bieber as our example. Take a look at his stat block: the first line and the **YEAR**, **TEAM**, **LVL** and **AGE** columns are the same as in the position player example earlier.

Here too, we have a series of columns that display raw, unadjusted statistics compiled by the pitcher over the course of a season: **W** (wins), **L** (losses), **SV** (saves), **G** (games pitched), **GS** (games started), **IP** (innings pitched), **H** (hits allowed) and **HR** (home runs allowed). Next we have two statistics that are rates: **BB/9** (walks per nine innings) and **K/9** (strikeouts per nine innings), before returning to the unadjusted K (strikeouts).

Next up is **GB%** (ground ball percentage), which is the percentage of all batted balls that were hit on the ground, including both outs and hits. Remember, this is based on observational data and subject to human error, so please approach this with a healthy dose of skepticism.

BABIP (batting average on balls in play) is calculated using the same methodology as it is for position players, but it often tells us more about a pitcher than it does a hitter. With pitchers, a high BABIP is often due to poor defense or bad luck, and can often be an indicator of potential rebound, and a low BABIP may be cause to expect performance regression. (A typical league-average BABIP is close to .290-.300.)

The metrics **WHIP** (walks plus hits per inning pitched) and **ERA** (earned run average) are old standbys: WHIP measures walks and hits allowed on a per-inning basis, while ERA measures earned runs on a nine-inning basis. Neither of these stats are translated or adjusted.

DRA- (Deserved Run Average) was described at length earlier, and measures how the pitcher "deserved" to perform compared to other pitchers. Please note that since we lack all the data points that would make for a "real" DRA for minor-league events, the DRA- displayed for minor league partial-seasons is based off of different data. (That data is a modified version of our cFIP metric, which you can find more information about on our website.)

Shane Bieber   RHP
Born: 05/31/95   Age: 26   Bats: R   Throws: R
Height: 6'3"   Weight: 200   Origin: Round 4, 2016 Draft (#122 overall)

YEAR	TEAM	LVL	AGE	W	L	SV	G	GS	IP	H	HR	BB/9	K/9	K	GB%	BABIP
2018	AKR	AA	23	3	0	0	5	5	31	26	1	0.3	8.7	30	47.3%	.278
2018	COL	AAA	23	3	1	0	8	8	48^2	30	3	1.1	8.7	47	52.0%	.227
2018	CLE	MLB	23	11	5	0	20	19	114^2	130	13	1.8	9.3	118	46.2%	.356
2019	CLE	MLB	24	15	8	0	34	33	214^1	186	31	1.7	10.9	259	44.4%	.298
2020	CLE	MLB	25	8	1	0	12	12	77^1	46	7	2.4	14.2	122	48.4%	.267
2021 FS	CLE	MLB	26	10	6	0	26	26	150	121	18	2.1	11.7	195	45.5%	.297
2021 DC	CLE	MLB	26	14	7	0	30	30	196.7	159	24	2.1	11.7	257	45.5%	.297

Comparables: Luis Severino, Danny Salazar, Joe Musgrove

YEAR	TEAM	LVL	AGE	WHIP	ERA	DRA-	WARP	MPH	FB%	WHF	CSP
2018	AKR	AA	23	0.87	1.16	61	0.9				
2018	COL	AAA	23	0.74	1.66	69	1.2				
2018	CLE	MLB	23	1.33	4.55	74	2.6	94.7	57.4%	26.2%	
2019	CLE	MLB	24	1.05	3.28	75	4.9	94.4	45.8%	30.8%	
2020	CLE	MLB	25	0.87	1.63	53	2.6	95.3	53.6%	40.7%	
2021 FS	CLE	MLB	26	1.04	2.44	64	4.4	94.7	50.0%	33.2%	44.2%
2021 DC	CLE	MLB	26	1.04	2.44	64	5.8	94.7	50.0%	33.2%	44.2%

Just like with hitters, **WARP** (Wins Above Replacement Player) is a total value metric that puts pitchers of all stripes on the same scale as position players. We use DRA as the primary input for our calculation of WARP. You might notice that relief pitchers (due to their limited innings) may have a lower WARP than you were expecting or than you might see in other WARP-like metrics. WARP does not take leverage into account, just the actions a pitcher performs and the expected value of those actions ... which ends up judging high-leverage relief pitchers differently than you might imagine given their prestige and market value.

MPH gives you the pitcher's 95th percentile velocity for the noted season, in order to give you an idea of what the *peak* fastball velocity a pitcher possesses. Since this comes from our pitch-tracking data, it is not publicly available for minor-league pitchers.

Finally, we display the three new pitching metrics we described earlier. **FB%** (fastball percentage) gives you the percentage of fastballs thrown out of all pitches. **WHF** (whiff rate) tells you the percentage of swinging strikes induced out of all pitches. **CSP** (called strike probability) expresses the likelihood of all pitches thrown to result in a called strike, after controlling for factors like handedness, umpire, pitch type, count and location.

PECOTA

All players have PECOTA projections for 2021, as well as a set of other numbers that describe the performance of comparable players according to PECOTA. All projections for 2021 are for the player at the date we went to press in early January and are projected into the league and park context as indicated by the team abbreviation. (Note that players at very low levels of the minors are too unpredictable to assess using these numbers.) All PECOTA projected statistics represent a player's projected major-league performance.

How we're doing that is a little different this season. There are really two different values that go into the final stat line that you see for PECOTA: How a player performs, and how much playing time he'll be given to perform it. In the past we've estimated playing time based on each team's roster and depth charts, and we'll continue to do that. These projections are denoted as **2021 DC**.

But in many cases, a player won't be projected for major-league playing time; most of the time this is because they aren't projected to be major-league players at all, but still developing as prospects. Or perhaps a player will provide Triple-A depth, only to have an opportunity open up because of injury. For these purposes, we're also supplying a second projection, labeled **2021 FS**, or full season. This is what we would project the player to provide in 600 plate appearances or 150 innings pitched.

Below the projections are the player's three highest-scoring comparable players as determined by PECOTA. All comparables represent a snapshot of how the listed player was performing at the same age as the current player, so if a

23-year-old pitcher is compared to Bartolo Colón, he's actually being compared to a 23-year-old Colón, not the version that pitched for the Rangers in 2018, nor to Colón's career as a whole.

A few points about pitcher projections. First, we aren't yet projecting peak velocity, so that column will be blank in the PECOTA lines. Second, projecting DRA is trickier than evaluating past performance, because it is unclear how deserving each pitcher will be of his anticipated outcomes. However, we know that another DRA-related statistic–contextual FIP or cFIP–estimates future run scoring very well. So for PECOTA, the projected DRA- figures you see are based on the past cFIPs generated by the pitcher and comparable players over time, along with the other factors described above.

If you're familiar with PECOTA, then you'll have noticed that the projection system often appears bullish on players coming off a bad year and bearish on players coming off a good year. (This is because the system weights several previous seasons, not just the most recent one.) In addition, we publish the 50th percentile projections for each player–which is smack in the middle of the range of projected production—which tends to mean PECOTA stat lines don't often have extreme results like 40 home runs or 250 strikeouts in a given season. In essence, PECOTA doesn't project very many extreme seasons.

Managers

After all those wonderful team chapters, we've got statistics for each big-league manager, all of whom are organized by alphabetical order. Here you'll find a block including an extraordinary amount of information collected from each manager's entire career. For more information on the acronyms and what they mean, please visit the Glossary at www.baseballprospectus.com.

There is one important metric that we'd like to call attention to, and you'll find it next to each manager's name: **wRM+** (weighted reliever management plus). Developed by Rob Arthur and Rian Watt, wRM+ investigates how good a manager is at using their best relievers during the moments of highest leverage, using both our proprietary DRA metric as well as Leverage Index. wRM+ is scaled to a league average of 100, and a wRM+ of 105 indicates that relievers were used approximately five percent "better" than average. On the other hand, a wRM+ of 95 would tell us the team used its relievers five percent "worse" than the average team.

While wRM+ does not have an extremely strong correlation with a manager, it is statistically significant; this means that a manager is not *entirely* responsible for a team's wRM+, but does have some effect on that number.

Part 1: Team Analysis

Performance Graphs

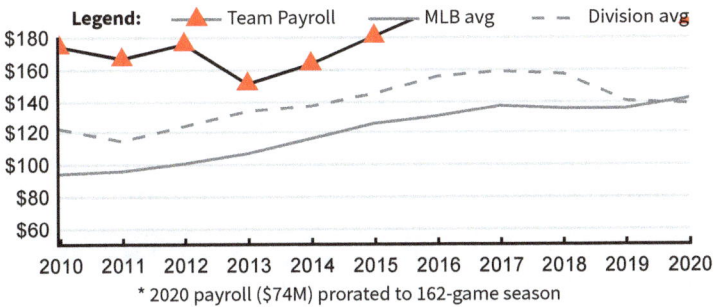

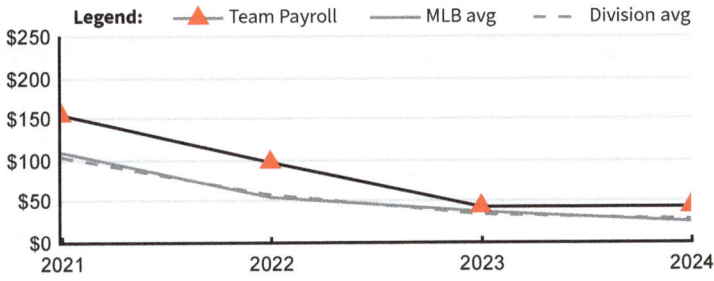

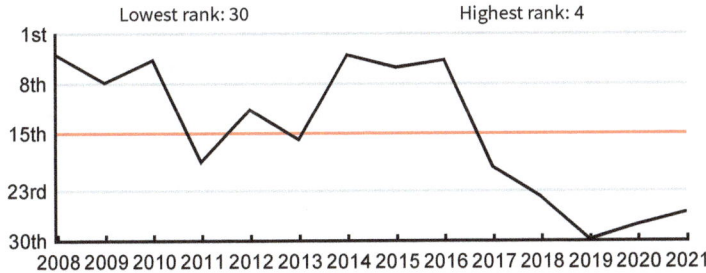

2020 Team Performance

ACTUAL STANDINGS

Team	W	L	Pct
TB	40	20	0.667
NYY	33	27	0.550
TOR	32	28	0.533
BAL	25	35	0.417
BOS	**24**	**36**	**0.400**

dWIN% STANDINGS

Team	W	L	Pct
NYY	33	27	0.560
TB	29	31	0.495
BOS	**25**	**35**	**0.429**
TOR	25	35	0.425
BAL	25	35	0.420

TOP HITTERS

Player	WARP
Christian Vázquez	1.2
Xander Bogaerts	0.9
Alex Verdugo	0.9

TOP PITCHERS

Player	WARP
Nathan Eovaldi	1.0
Ryan Brasier	0.4
Matt Barnes	0.4

VITAL STATISTICS

Statistic Name	Value	Rank
Pythagenpat	.410	26th
dWin%	.429	21st
Runs Scored per Game	4.87	11th
Runs Allowed per Game	5.85	29th
Deserved Runs Created Plus	95	19th
Deserved Run Average Minus	107	22nd
Fielding Independent Pitching	5.29	30th
Defensive Efficiency Rating	.648	30th
Batter Age	27.6	8th
Pitcher Age	29.2	24th
Payroll	$74.0M	5th
Marginal $ per Marginal Win	$9.4M	29th

2021 Team Projections

PROJECTED STANDINGS

Team	W	L	Pct	+/-
NYY	99.5	62.5	0.614	10
The starting rotation was loaded with risk even before Corey Kluber and Jameson Taillon became members. At least D.J. LeMahieu should keep the lineup humming.				
TB	86.0	76.0	0.531	-22
The defending AL champions didn't really spend their winter defending anything.				
TOR	84.4	77.6	0.521	-2
They stopped a starting pitcher short of credibly claiming favorite status, but adding George Springer gives them one of the junior circuit's most lethal lineups.				
BOS	**79.3**	**82.7**	**0.490**	**14**
There's a faint flavor of their 2012-13 offseason to what Boston did this winter, and look how that year turned out.				
BAL	66.1	95.9	0.408	-1
Mike Elias was forthright about his disinterest in winning in the short term. His winter proved he was serious.				

TOP PROJECTED HITTERS

Player	WARP
Xander Bogaerts	3.6
Christian Vázquez	2.6
Alex Verdugo	2.2

TOP PROJECTED PITCHERS

Player	WARP
Chris Sale	2.4
Eduardo Rodriguez	2.3
Nathan Eovaldi	2.2

FARM SYSTEM REPORT

Top Prospect	Number of Top 101 Prospects
Triston Casas, #85	1

KEY DEDUCTIONS

Player	WARP
Andrew Benintendi	1.5

KEY ADDITIONS

Player	WARP
Hunter Renfroe	1.7
Enrique Hernández	1.4
Matt Andriese	1.2
Franchy Cordero	1.2
Garrett Richards	1.1
Collin McHugh	0.9
Adam Ottavino	0.6
Hirokazu Sawamura	0.3

Team Personnel

Chief Baseball Officer
Chaim Bloom

Executive Vice President/Assistant General Manager
Raquel Ferreira

Vice President, Player Development
Ben Crockett

Manager
Alex Cora

BP Alumni
Chaim Bloom
Todd Gold
Jason Karegeannes

Fenway Park Stats

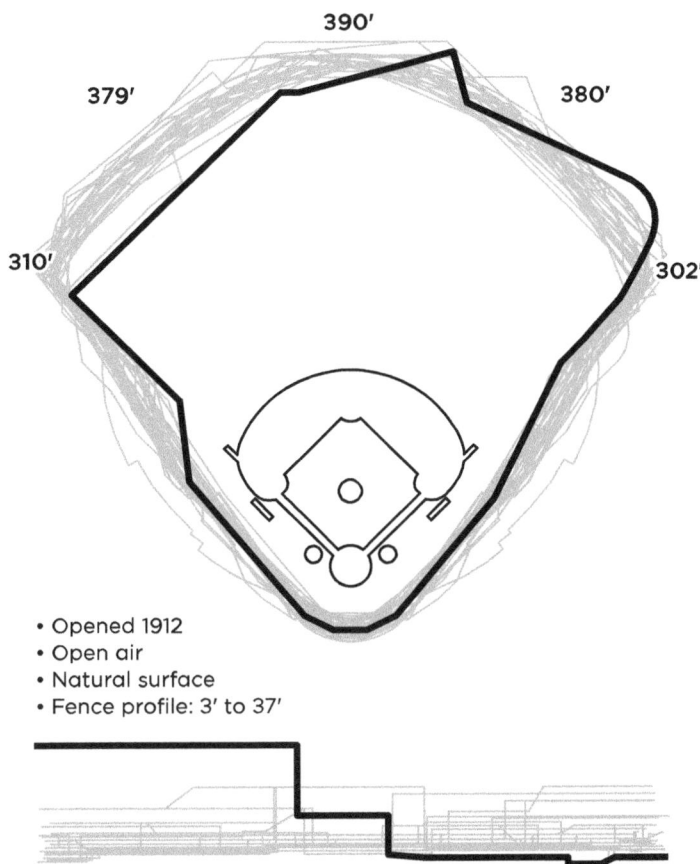

- Opened 1912
- Open air
- Natural surface
- Fence profile: 3' to 37'

Three-Year Park Factors

Runs	Runs/RH	Runs/LH	HR/RH	HR/LH
103	104	102	97	91

Red Sox Team Analysis

On September 1, the Red Sox sent a tweet from their official Twitter account that read "iykyk"—internet shorthand for "if you know, you know"—with an image of a hand about to press a blue "reset" button. The Sox owned a 12-23 record at the time but had achieved their goal for 2020: they had reset the luxury tax, and they wanted the world to know it. Sure, the team was terrible, and yes, they had reduced payroll by jettisoning one of the best players in franchise history. But John Henry—a man with an estimated net worth of nearly $3 billion—was set to save a few million dollars in baseball taxes. The real victory was in hand.

The tweet itself was not the issue, of course. It was merely the baseball equivalent of a Mission Accomplished banner hanging from an aircraft carrier two months into a war without purpose or end, a PR faux pas that perfectly encapsulated the cynicism and self-serving interests required to achieve such "victory" in the first place.

The issue is that the Boston Red Sox proudly announced to the world that they were no longer special.

After long serving as one of the last teams committed to spending their way to championships, the Sox have joined a growing majority of the league in their willingness to abdicate the chief responsibility assigned to a baseball team: to prioritize winning. Instead, Henry and co. now "worship at the altar of financial flexibility," as Jon Tayler so aptly warned would happen in this very space last year. With baseball teams increasingly able to divorce profits from performance, their directives have shifted from "win at all costs" to "win by cutting costs." If Mookie Betts would have to play Iphigenia to Henry's Agamemnon, so be it: the ends justify the means when the ends produce more ROI.

There are many reasons the Betts trade—or, perhaps more aptly, the Betts salary dump—is a baseball tragedy. It deprived the Red Sox of an otherworldly talent on pace to finish as its second-best player ever. It will forever stain the legacy of Henry, once one of baseball's better owners, and pushed new general manager Chaim Bloom into a role of pure villainy. It gutted the foundation of a team that had won 108 games and the World Series just a year earlier. And it turned the Boston Red Sox—a marquee franchise in the midst of their most successful era in franchise history—into yet another Modern Baseball Corporation: a bloated version of the Tampa Bay Rays or Pittsburgh Pirates with more resources but even less purpose or soul.

Through a Red Sox-colored lens it's tempting to say that there were no winners in the Mookie Betts trade, but in reality, the victors are obvious: the team that acquired him and Betts himself. Betts proved to be the piece the Dodgers needed to get over the World Series hump. His five-tool talents played just as well out west as they did back east, as evidenced by his second-place finish in NL MVP voting. Betts also won by refusing to accept below-market extension offers from the Red Sox. Instead, he inked a 12-year, $365 million deal with the Dodgers that rightly places him behind only Mike Trout in baseball's financial hierarchy. There were victors aplenty in this deal, but none of them are still employed by the Red Sox.

Now that Henry has watched his own team collapse and Betts win another ring, one has to wonder if he fully appreciated the extent to which the Betts trade would undermine his previous efforts. Before committing a baseball high crime, Henry had served as the best owner in Red Sox franchise history. Since he headlined a group that purchased the Red Sox for a then-record $700 million in 2001, Henry's Sox have finished in the top five in payroll all but once, and have placed first or second in spending nine times in 19 tries. He led the renovation of Fenway Park, keeping the Sox in downtown(ish) Boston and preserving a national landmark. It was under Henry that the Sox brought in Theo Epstein, a man who, for better and worse, would become the prototype of the modern baseball executive. He wrote Ben Cherington and Dave Dombrowski blank checks to pursue free agent mega-deals to mixed results. Most importantly, the Sox have won four World Series under Henry's reign after an 86-year drought of infamy.

But while Henry may seem golden compared to his predecessors and his peer set, that's in part because we hold the entire class of baseball owners to far too low a standard. Yes, Henry has spent big bucks on the Red Sox, but the $700 million "investment" he played a major role in securing back in 2001 is now worth an estimated $3.3 *billion*, per Forbes. Henry *should* be spending like crazy—has a mandate too, really—because his ownership of the Red Sox is a license to print money. For those looking to excuse Henry because COVID-19 killed fan attendance, consider that ticket sales make up an ever-shrinking portion of teams' revenue streams. What's more, it *is* actually possible for an ownership group to elect to suffer one season of financial loss amid decades of wild profits instead of transferring those losses down to personnel, players and the fan base. Once upon a time, Henry seemed like the type of owner willing to make such a decision. Now, he seems content to merely follow the crowd.

Though we're living through the death of nuance, Henry's stewardship deserves both praise and scorn. Yes, he's spent more than most owners, and yes, he's played an unquantifiable role in the Red Sox's resurgence of the past two decades. He should also be tried at The Baseball Hague for choosing to draw the financial line at *literally Mookie Betts*. Consider all the ancillary revenue streams he's built up thanks in part to the Red Sox: NESN, *The Boston Globe*, the

Fenway Sports Group and, most recently, its real estate subsidiary. Henry could blow past the luxury tax every year without meaningful consequence to his long-term profits. Perhaps you don't want to hold him to that standard, but surely he could've found a way to reduce his tax burden without evicting his franchise's best player.

That leads us to Bloom, Henry's latest choice to serve as architect of a Player Development Machine. Hailed as an innovator who'd deftly led the cash-strapped Rays to perennial relevance, Bloom's early moves in Boston have been as unimaginative as it gets. Trading your best, most expensive players for prospects is not novel or savvy: it is the type of obvious, cop-out "solution" every arm-chair GM deploys in their dynasty leagues. Perhaps Bloom had a mandate from ownership to move Betts, or at least a directive to get under the luxury tax at all costs. If the latter is true, there must have been other ways to do so rather than jettisoning one of the best players in franchise history for a collection of cheap but unproven talent. Is it not better to attach draft capital to Nate Eovaldi to get out from under his contract? To let Jackie Bradley Jr. go for a C-level prospect? To take 40 cents on the dollar for J.D. Martinez if the end result is Betts in Cooperstown with a Red Sox cap? We have no way of knowing if those moves were ever truly on the table, but all are individually *and* collectively preferable to trading Betts.

In large part, Red Sox Nation has recognized the Betts trade for what it is: an unmitigated disaster that benefits no one in New England but Henry. But as always, a smattering of contrarian takes persist. Some Sox fans proved so conditioned to side with ownership they cited the luxury tax as a burden. Some columnists remained so cynically contrarian they argued Betts' contract demands were simply too high. Worse yet was the vocal minority who insisted Betts was never going to sign in Boston long-term, steadfast in the type of reflexive defensiveness often seen from small-market fans who've watched their stars routinely leave for more lucrative pastures.

None of those arguments hold the slightest bit of water. A few million dollars in luxury tax should be a non-issue for a billionaire. To argue that the back-half of Betts' mega-deal may not offer surplus value ignores that the first-half that will—already has, if you recall who just won the World Series—and, if taken to its logical conclusion, suggests teams should never engage with top-flight free agents: another pro-ownership argument. And the only evidence we have that Betts did not want to be in Boston long-term was his unwillingness to accept below-market extension overtures earlier in his career. In fact, Betts himself has said that for a long time, he expected to retire a Red Sox.

There's one more pro-trade argument even more disingenuous than the rest: that it was a good *baseball* move, allowing the Red Sox to get younger and cheaper, to diversify their risk. One needs only contrast Boston's dumpster fire of a 2020 season with the Dodgers' soaring success to put that notion to rest. The haul the Red Sox received for Betts and fellow star David Price included some interesting long-term pieces. Alex Verdugo impressed in his first run as Betts' replacement. The ironically named Jeter Downs is a fine prospect. The Betts trade was not quite so lop-sided as the Ruthian transaction to which it's often compared. But make no mistake about it: it was an abject disaster for the Red Sox on the diamond. It was only a win for Henry's bottom line.

It's tempting for Red Sox fans to drown in a sea of "what-if," but the cold, hard truth is that Betts' departure leaves the Red Sox in an odd state of quasi-contention, "burdened" with too much talent to truly tank over a full season but lacking the pitching needed for a serious run. Xander Bogaerts, Rafael Devers and Verdugo comprise one of the league's better young offensive cores, and the Sox now have some life on the farm thanks to Downs, Triston Casas and others. But this is an organization woefully short on arms even *if* Chris Sale and Eduardo Rodriguez return to health. With a Betts-like talent in tow, perhaps the Sox could've pried their contention cycle open with an otherworldly offense, banking on Bloom's track record of unearthing live arms to patch the holes. Instead, they're purposely entering baseball purgatory, more likely to win 81 games than 65 or 95.

That seems to be the way Henry wants it now. There are legitimate reasons to seek an end to the peaks and valleys the Red Sox have experienced of late: in the past seven seasons, Boston has finished first in the division three times, last three times, and third once. There's an argument to be made in favor of shaving some upside for a higher yearly floor. But it's hard to look at the Betts trade and believe the primary motivator was anything other than saving ownership some cash. Betts represented the single most valuable type of commodity in baseball: a homegrown megastar in his prime without flaws on or off the field. If you really want to compete year-in and year-out, that's the guy you build around, and you figure out the rest. Instead, Sox fans are left only with empty platitudes about "financial flexibility" and "sustainability" as Henry, Tom Werner and co. deploy Bloom and CEO Sam Kennedy as human shields at press conferences, refusing to answer directly for their baseball sins.

Perhaps this all seems a bit dramatic. The Red Sox are hardly the first team to trade a superstar, and they won't be the last. But the Sox haven't just lost Betts; they've lost their identity. Despite a deserved reputation for smearing players on the way out of town, the Sox also had a penchant for taking care of their own. Franchise icons and homegrown heroes such as Jason Varitek, Tim Wakefield, Dustin Pedroia and, of course, David Ortiz, were essentially given lifetime contracts. When others like Jon Lester were shown the door, there were at least credible baseball justifications for their departures. The Sox were an organization that *hoarded* stars: not one that shed them to save a few bucks.

That's no longer the case. Betts will end his career with the Dodgers because Henry has decided he'd rather his team be profitable than good, efficient than special. And if you really need more evidence that baseball is broken than the *Boston Red Sox* trading *Mookie Betts*, just wait a season or two: some other "big-market team" will soon follow suit. The altar of financial flexibility is always hungry for another sacrifice.

—*Ben Carsley is an author of Baseball Prospectus.*

Part 2: Player Analysis

PLAYER COMMENTS WITH GRAPHS

Jonathan Araúz   SS
Born: 08/03/98   Age: 22   Bats: S   Throws: R
Height: 6'0"   Weight: 195   Origin: International Free Agent, 2014

YEAR	TEAM	LVL	AGE	PA	R	2B	3B	HR	RBI	BB	K	SB	CS	AVG/OBP/SLG
2018	QC	LO-A	19	237	31	11	6	4	29	30	38	7	6	.299/.392/.471
2018	FAY	HI-A	19	253	25	10	3	4	18	16	36	1	2	.167/.223/.288
2019	FAY	HI-A	20	354	41	19	0	8	42	30	69	5	4	.252/.322/.388
2019	CC	AA	20	119	12	3	2	3	13	10	19	1	1	.241/.311/.389
2020	BOS	MLB	21	80	8	2	0	1	9	8	21	0	0	.250/.325/.319
2021 FS	BOS	MLB	22	600	66	23	2	13	57	50	156	2	2	.219/.289/.349
2021 DC	BOS	MLB	22	60	6	2	0	1	5	5	15	0	0	.219/.289/.349

Comparables: Domingo Leyba, Gavin Cecchini, Marwin Gonzalez

Look, fielding a competitive roster has its advantages—sometimes it even results in a World Series win—but the downside of competing is that you never get the chance to roster guys like Arauz. Popped with the 17th pick in the 2019 Rule 5 draft, Arauz came to Boston via Houston with a reputation as a glove-first middle infielder with some feel for making contact. He played as advertised, making cameos all across the infield while posting a DRC+ just below league average. That modest combination of skills combined with expanded rosters and Boston's exodus of talent let Arauz hang around on the roster all season, which means the Sox can now stash him in the minors for a few more years. It seems like that's maybe not worth nuking your franchise over, but hey—there's some real potential for surplus value here, and that's what the new Red Sox are all about.

YEAR	TEAM	LVL	AGE	PA	DRC+	BABIP	BRR	FRAA	WARP
2018	QC	LO-A	19	237	147	.350	0.4	SS(33): 0.6, 2B(17): 0.4, 3B(3): -0.3	1.9
2018	FAY	HI-A	19	253	38	.180	-2.6	SS(70): -5.5, 2B(1): -0.1	-2.0
2019	FAY	HI-A	20	354	110	.296	-2.5	SS(62): -2.3, 3B(18): 0.8, 2B(6): 0.0	1.3
2019	CC	AA	20	119	118	.267	-0.8	2B(15): -1.7, SS(7): 0.4, 3B(6): 0.2	0.4
2020	BOS	MLB	21	80	76	.340	0.3	2B(16): -1.7, 3B(6): -0.3, SS(4): 0.6	-0.1
2021 FS	BOS	MLB	22	600	76	.281	-0.4	SS 0, 2B -2	-0.3
2021 DC	BOS	MLB	22	60	76	.281	0.0	SS 0, 2B 0	0.0

Jonathan Araúz, continued

Batted Ball Distribution

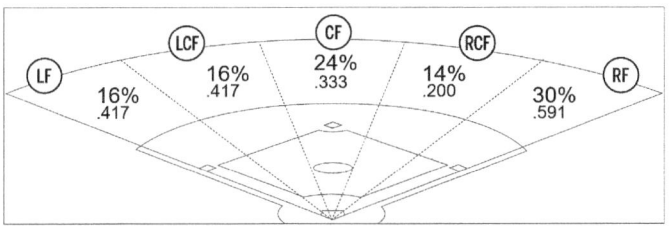

Strike Zone vs LHP   Strike Zone vs RHP

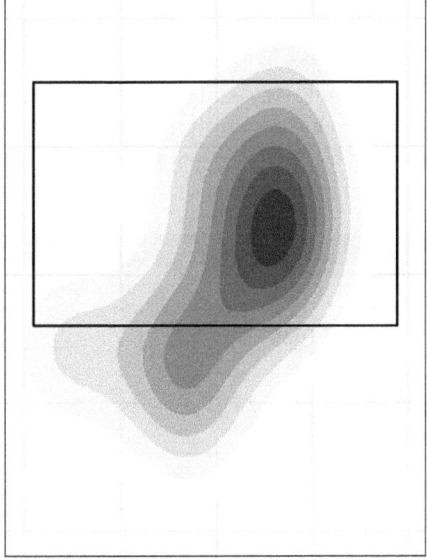

Christian Arroyo 3B

Born: 05/30/95 Age: 26 Bats: R Throws: R
Height: 6'1" Weight: 210 Origin: Round 1, 2013 Draft (#25 overall)

YEAR	TEAM	LVL	AGE	PA	R	2B	3B	HR	RBI	BB	K	SB	CS	AVG/OBP/SLG
2018	DUR	AAA	23	182	19	12	0	2	20	8	32	2	3	.235/.286/.341
2018	TB	MLB	23	59	5	2	1	1	6	6	16	0	0	.264/.339/.396
2019	DUR	AAA	24	134	21	9	1	8	29	12	26	1	0	.314/.381/.603
2019	TB	MLB	24	57	8	2	0	2	7	5	18	0	0	.220/.304/.380
2020	CLE	MLB	25	0	0	0	0	0	0	0	0	0	0	None/None/None
2020	BOS	MLB	25	54	7	1	0	3	8	4	11	0	0	.240/.296/.440
2021 FS	BOS	MLB	26	600	67	27	1	18	64	38	145	1	1	.238/.296/.392
2021 DC	BOS	MLB	26	125	14	5	0	3	13	8	30	0	0	.238/.296/.392

Comparables: Colin Moran, Christian Villanueva, Brian Barden

Get you a man who looks at you the way Chaim Bloom looks at Arroyo. Way back in 2017, Bloom was a senior VP of baseball ops with the Rays when they traded the face of their franchise Evan Longoria to the Giants for a package headlined by Arroyo, who was then a top prospect. It cost Bloom far less to acquire Arroyo the second time around given that Cleveland DFA'd him in August. With the Sox, Arroyo showed just enough defensive versatility and power to prove intriguing without hitting well enough to engender any real excitement. He's still young-ish and he's mashed at Triple-A, but is best viewed as a bench piece with a dash of upside. If nothing else, Red Sox fans are used to rooting for an Arroyo on the periphery of the roster, though hopefully this one refrains from cornrows.

YEAR	TEAM	LVL	AGE	PA	DRC+	BABIP	BRR	FRAA	WARP
2018	DUR	AAA	23	182	73	.279	1.0	3B(34): -1.2, SS(6): -0.2	-0.2
2018	TB	MLB	23	59	85	.361	0.4	2B(8): -0.5, 3B(7): -0.5	0.0
2019	DUR	AAA	24	134	143	.345	1.2	3B(20): 0.3, SS(9): -0.1, 2B(1): 0.1	1.3
2019	TB	MLB	24	57	72	.300	0.1	3B(13): -0.4, 2B(1): 0.0	0.0
2020	CLE	MLB	25	0				3B(1): -0.0	
2020	BOS	MLB	25	54	94	.250	0.8	2B(13): 3.8, SS(2): -0.2	0.6
2021 FS	BOS	MLB	26	600	89	.290	-0.8	2B 8, 3B 0	1.2
2021 DC	BOS	MLB	26	125	89	.290	-0.2	2B 2, 3B 0	0.3

Christian Arroyo, continued

Batted Ball Distribution

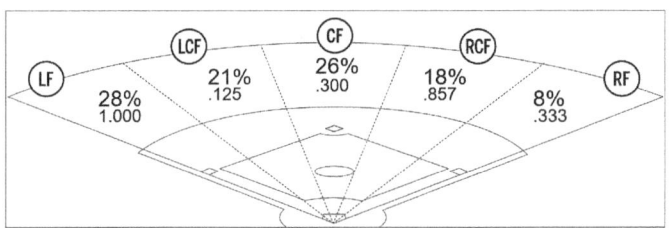

Strike Zone vs LHP   Strike Zone vs RHP

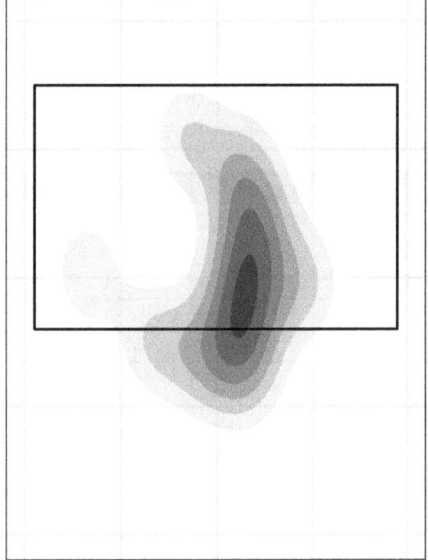

Xander Bogaerts SS

Born: 10/01/92 Age: 28 Bats: R Throws: R
Height: 6'2" Weight: 218 Origin: International Free Agent, 2009

YEAR	TEAM	LVL	AGE	PA	R	2B	3B	HR	RBI	BB	K	SB	CS	AVG/OBP/SLG
2018	BOS	MLB	25	580	72	45	3	23	103	55	102	8	2	.288/.360/.522
2019	BOS	MLB	26	698	110	52	0	33	117	76	122	4	2	.309/.384/.555
2020	BOS	MLB	27	225	36	8	0	11	28	21	41	8	0	.300/.364/.502
2021 FS	BOS	MLB	28	600	82	33	1	22	83	55	116	8	3	.281/.353/.475
2021 DC	BOS	MLB	28	591	81	32	1	22	82	54	114	7	3	.281/.353/.475

Comparables: Asdrúbal Cabrera, Rico Petrocelli, Khalil Greene

Bogaerts is a bona fide star flirting with a Hall of Fame career path, yet he's often been outshone by otherworldly talents. With Mookie Betts gone, Rafael Devers struggling and Chris Sale hurt, it was finally Bogey's show in 2020, and he looked mighty comfortable in the starring role. In addition to pacing the Sox in DRC+, homers, steals and runs scored, Bogaerts ranked in the top-10 among all shortstops in said categories. For once, FRAA agreed with the eye test and labeled him a fine if unremarkable defender, and he became a more vocal clubhouse leader in Betts' absence. The X-Man is a steadying presence for a franchise in turmoil, and the six-year, $120 million extension he signed in 2019 continues to look like a steal for the only org he's ever known. Bogaerts has an opt out after 2022, though, and while the market doesn't look great for free agents at present, neither do the Red Sox.

YEAR	TEAM	LVL	AGE	PA	DRC+	BABIP	BRR	FRAA	WARP
2018	BOS	MLB	25	580	130	.317	-0.2	SS(136): 1.5	4.9
2019	BOS	MLB	26	698	134	.338	-0.1	SS(153): -20.8	4.3
2020	BOS	MLB	27	225	113	.329	1.1	SS(53): -1.4	0.9
2021 FS	BOS	MLB	28	600	127	.322	-0.2	SS -3	3.7
2021 DC	BOS	MLB	28	591	127	.322	-0.2	SS -2	3.6

Xander Bogaerts, continued

Batted Ball Distribution

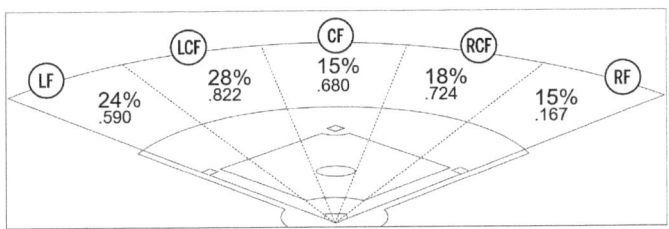

Strike Zone vs LHP   Strike Zone vs RHP

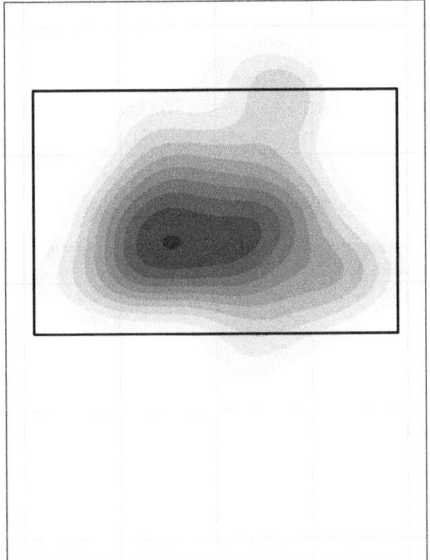

Jackie Bradley Jr. CF

Born: 04/19/90   Age: 31   Bats: L   Throws: R
Height: 5'10"   Weight: 196   Origin: Round 1, 2011 Draft (#40 overall)

YEAR	TEAM	LVL	AGE	PA	R	2B	3B	HR	RBI	BB	K	SB	CS	AVG/OBP/SLG
2018	BOS	MLB	28	535	76	33	4	13	59	46	137	17	1	.234/.314/.403
2019	BOS	MLB	29	567	69	28	3	21	62	56	155	8	6	.225/.317/.421
2020	BOS	MLB	30	217	32	11	0	7	22	23	48	5	2	.283/.364/.450
2021 FS	BOS	MLB	31	600	66	30	3	17	69	61	152	10	4	.239/.331/.410
2021 DC	BOS	MLB	31	475	52	23	2	14	55	48	120	8	3	.239/.331/.410

Comparables: B.J. Upton, Chris Young, Drew Stubbs

Few players embodied the last decade of Red Sox baseball quite like Bradley Jr. and his soaring peaks and low, low valleys. During his time in Boston, Bradley won two World Series rings, an ALCS MVP, made an All-Star team and earned a Gold Glove (and deserved a half-dozen more). He was also a below-average hitter for five of those eight seasons, was benched or platooned a handful of times and played on three last-place teams. A homegrown talent who somehow both under- and over-performed his prospect projections, he spoiled Red Sox fans with his otherworldly defense in center and spoiled appetites with months-long cold streaks at the plate interspersed with inexplicable stretches of dominance. Now entering his age-31 season, Bradley is coming off a strong walk year and makes sense for competitors looking for cost-effective options in center. In theory the Red Sox should fit that description, but it seems likely they'll let Bradley be the latest high-profile departure from a core that won 108 games just two years ago.

YEAR	TEAM	LVL	AGE	PA	DRC+	BABIP	BRR	FRAA	WARP
2018	BOS	MLB	28	535	87	.299	2.5	CF(135): 6.1, RF(15): 0.3	1.9
2019	BOS	MLB	29	567	86	.281	0.9	CF(144): 0.9, RF(3): 0.4	1.3
2020	BOS	MLB	30	217	94	.343	1.5	CF(55): -3.0	0.2
2021 FS	BOS	MLB	31	600	103	.304	0.5	CF 3, RF 0	2.5
2021 DC	BOS	MLB	31	475	103	.304	0.4	CF 2, RF 0	2.0

Jackie Bradley Jr., continued

Batted Ball Distribution

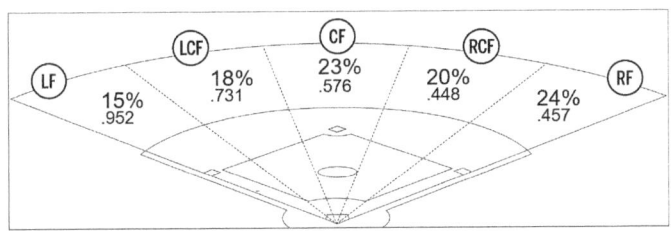

Strike Zone vs LHP

Strike Zone vs RHP

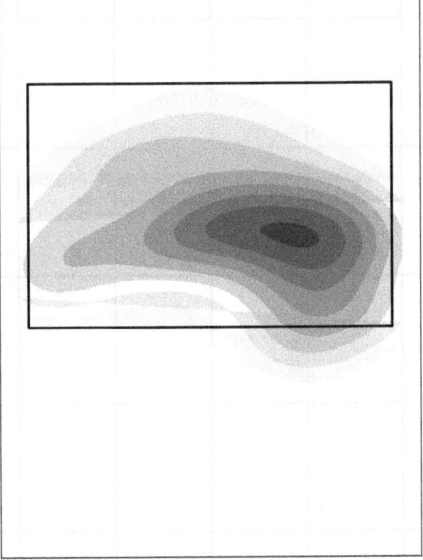

Michael Chavis 2B

Born: 08/11/95 Age: 25 Bats: R Throws: R
Height: 5'10" Weight: 210 Origin: Round 1, 2014 Draft (#26 overall)

YEAR	TEAM	LVL	AGE	PA	R	2B	3B	HR	RBI	BB	K	SB	CS	AVG/OBP/SLG
2018	POR	AA	22	139	23	7	0	6	17	13	35	3	1	.303/.388/.508
2018	WOR	AAA	22	34	8	3	0	2	7	1	12	0	0	.273/.294/.545
2019	WOR	AAA	23	79	11	4	0	7	11	8	21	0	0	.257/.329/.614
2019	BOS	MLB	23	382	46	10	1	18	58	31	127	2	1	.254/.322/.444
2020	BOS	MLB	24	158	16	5	2	5	19	8	50	3	0	.212/.259/.377
2021 FS	BOS	MLB	25	600	70	25	1	24	73	43	199	1	1	.228/.294/.417
2021 DC	BOS	MLB	25	316	37	13	1	12	38	22	104	0	1	.228/.294/.417

Comparables: Carlos Pena, Tony Clark, Jeff Clement

Chavis had a chance to prove he should be considered a foundational piece of the Next Good Red Sox team. Instead he played a role in Boston's collapse. Despite lucking into as clear a path to playing time as he could have possibly hoped for after an uneven rookie campaign, Chavis was unable to prove he belonged in the lineup every day. His strikeout rate remained sky-high while his walk and homer rates fell, and as the season progressed Chavis lost playing time to the bigger, better version of himself: rookie Bobby Dalbec. Chavis still has plus power and just enough defensive versatility to pique your interest, but it's clear that any team with first-division aspirations can't rely on him as their Plan A in any capacity.

YEAR	TEAM	LVL	AGE	PA	DRC+	BABIP	BRR	FRAA	WARP
2018	POR	AA	22	139	144	.383	0.5	3B(18): 1.5, 1B(10): -0.5	1.0
2018	WOR	AAA	22	34	90	.368	0.2	3B(4): -1.2, 1B(1): -0.0	-0.1
2019	WOR	AAA	23	79	142	.256	-0.7	2B(7): 1.6, 3B(7): -0.6, 1B(4): 0.9	0.7
2019	BOS	MLB	23	382	93	.347	0.0	1B(49): 2.4, 2B(45): -0.9, 3B(5): -0.2	0.7
2020	BOS	MLB	24	158	70	.280	-0.8	1B(24): 1.0, LF(12): -0.5, 2B(8): -0.5	-0.3
2021 FS	BOS	MLB	25	600	96	.308	-0.7	LF -4, 1B 1	0.5
2021 DC	BOS	MLB	25	316	96	.308	-0.4	LF -2, 1B 0	0.2

Michael Chavis, continued

Batted Ball Distribution

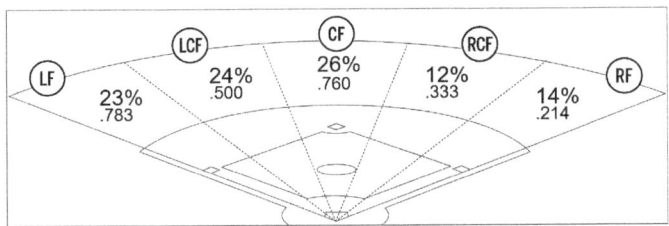

Strike Zone vs LHP

Strike Zone vs RHP

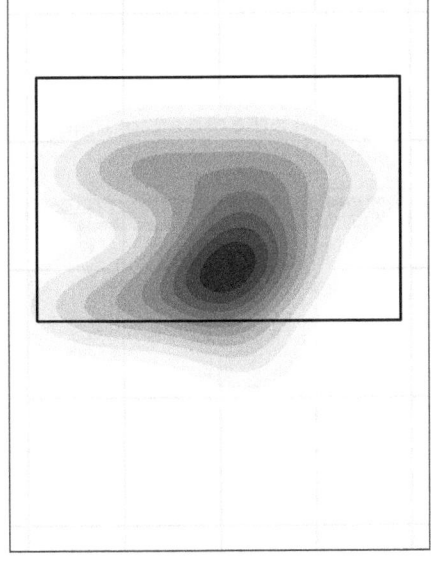

Bobby Dalbec 3B

Born: 06/29/95   Age: 26   Bats: R   Throws: R
Height: 6'4"   Weight: 227   Origin: Round 4, 2016 Draft (#118 overall)

YEAR	TEAM	LVL	AGE	PA	R	2B	3B	HR	RBI	BB	K	SB	CS	AVG/OBP/SLG
2018	SAL	HI-A	23	419	59	27	2	26	85	60	130	3	1	.256/.372/.573
2018	POR	AA	23	124	14	8	1	6	24	6	46	0	0	.261/.323/.514
2019	POR	AA	24	439	57	15	2	20	57	68	110	6	4	.234/.371/.454
2019	WOR	AAA	24	123	12	4	0	7	16	5	29	0	2	.257/.301/.478
2020	BOS	MLB	25	92	13	3	0	8	16	10	39	0	0	.263/.359/.600
2021 FS	BOS	MLB	26	600	77	23	1	26	75	56	239	1	1	.210/.296/.409
2021 DC	BOS	MLB	26	471	60	18	1	20	59	44	188	1	1	.210/.296/.409

Comparables: Mat Gamel, Matt Carpenter, Mike Olt

Sometimes prospects can fool you with their early major-league performance. Not so with Dalbec—he showed his true colors from day one. With his broad shoulders and vicious upper-cut swing, Dalbec provides true top-of-the-scale power and the potential to go bridge in every at-bat. But he'll need to dramatically cut back on his strikeouts in order to maximize his pop, and while he improved his approach in the upper minors, his 40-plus percent K rate in the majors is untenable. More often than not, this profile forces a player into a Quad-A or bench bat role. But for every dozen-or-so sluggers who are felled by such an extreme approach, a Joey Gallo emerges and does just enough to make it work. That's the dream for Dalbec, who possesses one more Gallo-ian trait: an absolute firehose of an arm.

YEAR	TEAM	LVL	AGE	PA	DRC+	BABIP	BRR	FRAA	WARP
2018	SAL	HI-A	23	419	159	.318	0.9	3B(91): 5.2, SS(1): 0.0	3.8
2018	POR	AA	23	124	96	.377	-0.1	3B(18): -3.9, 1B(2): -0.3	-0.4
2019	POR	AA	24	439	150	.278	-2.2	3B(90): 7.2, 1B(13): 0.9	4.2
2019	WOR	AAA	24	123	83	.278	0.3	3B(17): 2.0, 1B(11): -1.3	0.2
2020	BOS	MLB	25	92	92	.394	-0.2	1B(21): 1.8, 3B(2): -0.2	0.2
2021 FS	BOS	MLB	26	600	95	.318	-0.8	1B 0, 3B 0	0.7
2021 DC	BOS	MLB	26	471	95	.318	-0.6	1B 0	0.3

Bobby Dalbec, continued

Batted Ball Distribution

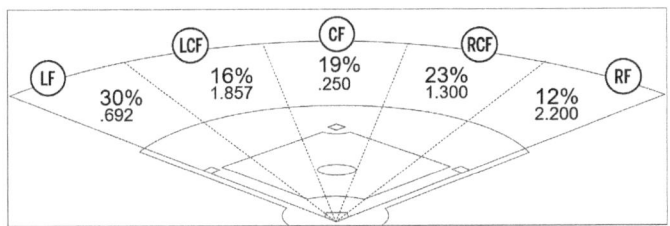

Strike Zone vs LHP   Strike Zone vs RHP

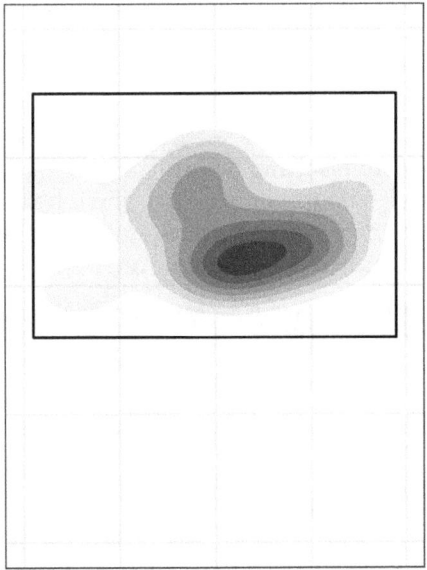

Rafael Devers 3B

Born: 10/24/96 Age: 24 Bats: L Throws: R
Height: 6'0" Weight: 240 Origin: International Free Agent, 2013

YEAR	TEAM	LVL	AGE	PA	R	2B	3B	HR	RBI	BB	K	SB	CS	AVG/OBP/SLG
2018	BOS	MLB	21	490	59	24	0	21	66	38	121	5	2	.240/.298/.433
2019	BOS	MLB	22	702	129	54	4	32	115	48	118	8	8	.311/.361/.555
2020	BOS	MLB	23	248	32	16	1	11	43	13	67	0	0	.263/.310/.483
2021 FS	BOS	MLB	24	600	81	33	3	24	78	43	152	5	3	.255/.314/.461
2021 DC	BOS	MLB	24	605	82	33	3	24	78	43	153	5	3	.255/.314/.461

Comparables: Will Middlebrooks, Hank Blalock, Travis Fryman

If 2019 represented two giant steps forward for Devers, 2020 marked a half-step back. The cherubic slugger hit just .182/.241/.325 through the season's first 20 games while reverting to oft-erratic play at third base. He eventually righted the ship at the plate, hitting .301/.345/.522 over the later two-thirds of Boston's lost season, but still placed just 34th in DRC+ among third basemen—24 spots worse than a year earlier. Devers' talent, age and track record remain points in his favor, but two recurring flaws threaten to stay his ascent to stardom: his troubles against left-handers and his wildness in the field. He hit just .222 against southpaws, albeit in 81 plate appearances, and posted the second-worst FRAA of any third baseman. Both maladies seemed remedied in 2019 but plagued Devers earlier in his career, which makes it tougher to chalk them up to small samples. As such, Devers' upcoming campaign should go a long way toward resolving two outstanding questions about his future: can he stick at third base through his 20s, and is he a merely good hitter or a truly great one? With extension talks and late arbitration years looming, tens of millions of dollars likely hinge on the answers.

YEAR	TEAM	LVL	AGE	PA	DRC+	BABIP	BRR	FRAA	WARP
2018	BOS	MLB	21	490	94	.281	1.7	3B(116): 11.2	2.8
2019	BOS	MLB	22	702	124	.339	0.2	3B(152): 7.2, SS(1): -0.0	5.6
2020	BOS	MLB	23	248	95	.325	1.1	3B(57): -8.7	-0.4
2021 FS	BOS	MLB	24	600	109	.311	0.0	3B 1, SS 0	2.0
2021 DC	BOS	MLB	24	605	109	.311	0.0	3B 1	2.0

Rafael Devers, continued

Batted Ball Distribution

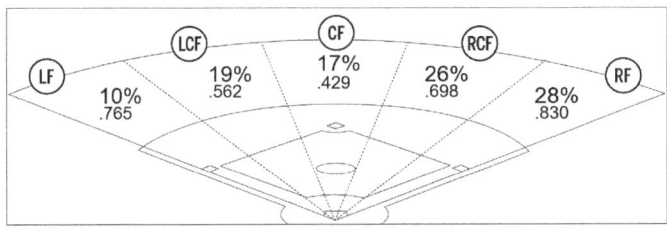

Strike Zone vs LHP   Strike Zone vs RHP

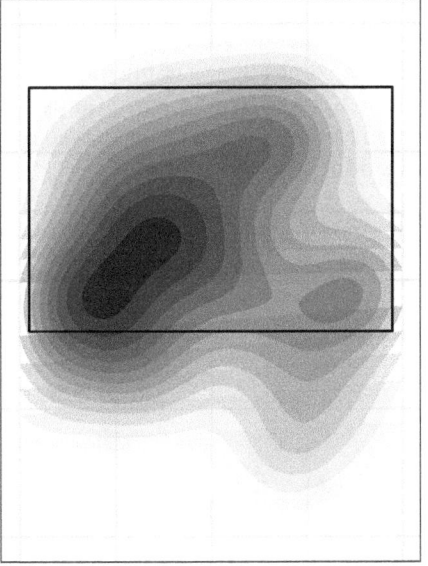

Enrique Hernández 2B

Born: 08/24/91 Age: 29 Bats: R Throws: R
Height: 5'11" Weight: 190 Origin: Round 6, 2009 Draft (#191 overall)

YEAR	TEAM	LVL	AGE	PA	R	2B	3B	HR	RBI	BB	K	SB	CS	AVG/OBP/SLG
2018	LAD	MLB	26	462	67	17	3	21	52	50	78	2	0	.256/.336/.470
2019	LAD	MLB	27	460	57	19	1	17	64	36	97	4	0	.237/.304/.411
2020	LAD	MLB	28	148	20	8	1	5	20	6	31	0	1	.230/.270/.410
2021 FS	BOS	MLB	29	600	71	28	1	20	68	53	140	3	2	.232/.306/.405
2021 DC	BOS	MLB	29	539	64	25	1	18	61	48	125	3	1	.232/.306/.405

Comparables: Geronimo Pena, Jason Kipnis, Jeff Kent

If you catch yourself saying that many players are worth substantially more or less to their team than WARP shows, you're probably letting subjectivity govern your evaluations too much. If you can't identify the occasional case in which that's true, though, you err in the other direction, and you risk misunderstanding baseball as a mere game of digital tallies. Hernández excels in every area which we still can't objectively measure well. He not only plays all over the diamond, but is above-average in just about every spot. He brings levity to the clubhouse, moves freely between what might otherwise become cliques, and still puts in the work required to be a consistent player on the field. He also comes up big in big moments, with a career .827 OPS when the game is within a run of being tied. In Game 7 of the NLCS, the Dodgers were within a run when Hernández pinch-hit to lead off the bottom of the sixth inning. When he was done, they were tied.

YEAR	TEAM	LVL	AGE	PA	DRC+	BABIP	BRR	FRAA	WARP
2018	LAD	MLB	26	462	112	.266	1.9	CF(63): -0.8, 2B(41): -0.3, SS(22): -1.3	2.2
2019	LAD	MLB	27	460	91	.266	1.3	2B(85): 1.1, CF(20): -1.4, RF(17): 0.3	1.1
2020	LAD	MLB	28	148	93	.260	0.2	2B(30): 3.9, RF(9): -0.6, LF(5): 0.7	0.7
2021 FS	BOS	MLB	29	600	96	.276	-0.5	2B 1, RF 2	1.7
2021 DC	BOS	MLB	29	539	96	.276	-0.5	2B 1, RF 1	1.4

Enrique Hernández, continued

Batted Ball Distribution

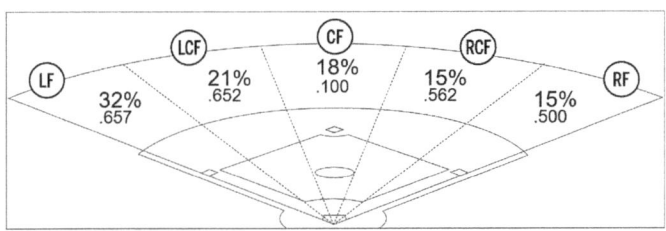

Strike Zone vs LHP   Strike Zone vs RHP

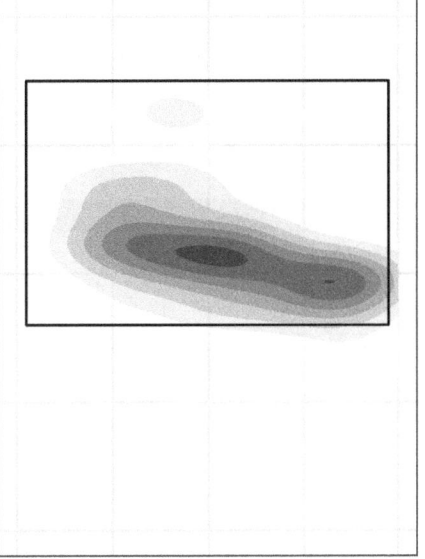

J.D. Martinez LF

Born: 08/21/87 Age: 33 Bats: R Throws: R
Height: 6'3" Weight: 230 Origin: Round 20, 2009 Draft (#611 overall)

YEAR	TEAM	LVL	AGE	PA	R	2B	3B	HR	RBI	BB	K	SB	CS	AVG/OBP/SLG
2018	BOS	MLB	30	649	111	37	2	43	130	69	146	6	1	.330/.402/.629
2019	BOS	MLB	31	657	98	33	2	36	105	72	138	2	0	.304/.383/.557
2020	BOS	MLB	32	237	22	16	0	7	27	22	59	1	0	.213/.291/.389
2021 FS	BOS	MLB	33	600	81	27	1	26	81	59	162	2	2	.246/.326/.453
2021 DC	BOS	MLB	33	605	81	27	1	27	82	60	164	2	2	.246/.326/.453

Comparables: Jay Buhner, Nelson Cruz, Ryan Ludwick

There are three main reasons Martinez elected not to opt out of his contract, in essence settling for a two-year, ~$39 million deal to remain with the Red Sox. First, COVID-19 wreaked havoc on baseball's economy, with owners all too eager to ensure players feel the pain of lower profit margins. Second, MLB opted against adopting a universal DH, effectively halving Martinez's market. And third—and perhaps most importantly—Martinez flat-out stunk in 2020. One year after finishing 15th in the majors in DRC+, Martinez hit worse than Ty France and Brandon Crawford, posting his worst offensive output since 2013. It's reasonably safe to assume that Martinez's sudden belly flop stemmed from a small sample on a lifeless team in a weird season. That being said, Martinez is now a 33-year-old DH with declining bat speed who spent more time complaining about the lack of in-game video than he did on base last season. A bounce back is likely, yes, but far from guaranteed.

YEAR	TEAM	LVL	AGE	PA	DRC+	BABIP	BRR	FRAA	WARP
2018	BOS	MLB	30	649	166	.375	-3.9	LF(32): -0.9, RF(25): 2.4	6.3
2019	BOS	MLB	31	657	138	.342	-6.2	RF(24): 3.8, LF(15): 0.5	4.2
2020	BOS	MLB	32	237	97	.259	-1.5	RF(4): -0.8, LF(3): 0.4	0.2
2021 FS	BOS	MLB	33	600	114	.302	-0.7	LF 0, RF 0	2.4
2021 DC	BOS	MLB	33	605	114	.302	-0.7	LF 0	2.1

J.D. Martinez, continued

Batted Ball Distribution

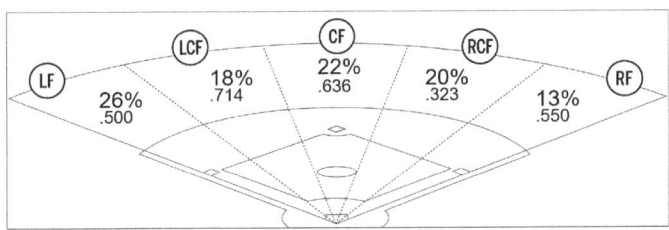

Strike Zone vs LHP   Strike Zone vs RHP

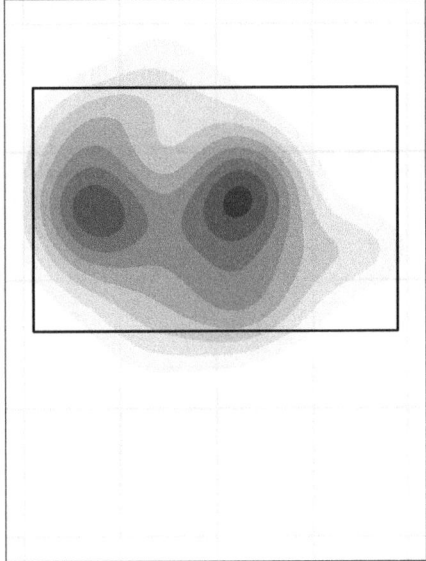

Yairo Muñoz OF

Born: 01/23/95 Age: 26 Bats: R Throws: R
Height: 5'11" Weight: 200 Origin: International Free Agent, 2012

YEAR	TEAM	LVL	AGE	PA	R	2B	3B	HR	RBI	BB	K	SB	CS	AVG/OBP/SLG
2018	MEM	AAA	23	100	11	3	1	3	13	5	18	1	0	.287/.330/.436
2018	STL	MLB	23	329	39	16	0	8	42	30	71	5	6	.276/.350/.413
2019	STL	MLB	24	181	20	7	1	2	13	7	37	8	3	.267/.298/.355
2020	BOS	MLB	25	45	6	5	0	1	4	0	11	2	0	.333/.333/.511
2021 FS	BOS	MLB	26	600	67	28	1	16	64	34	140	9	5	.249/.298/.398
2021 DC	BOS	MLB	26	32	3	1	0	0	3	1	7	0	0	.249/.298/.398

Comparables: Bobby Crosby, Addison Russell, Rico Petrocelli

Muñoz started his 2020 season by fulfilling a fantasy that many a baseball fan has had over the years: walking out on the St. Louis Cardinals. After suffering a hamstring injury in late February, Muñoz took an unsanctioned flight back to his native Dominican Republic and refused to return the Cardinals' calls. That prompted a DFA, which allowed the Sox to scoop him up on a minor-league deal a few weeks later. In his limited action in Boston, he was the same guy as in St. Louis: a good hitter with pop but no real defensive home. The Sox have stockpiled such players as of late, so Muñoz figures to face stiff competition for a lasting supersub role. Hopefully he won't walk away from such a chance this time around.

YEAR	TEAM	LVL	AGE	PA	DRC+	BABIP	BRR	FRAA	WARP
2018	MEM	AAA	23	100	104	.329	0.3	SS(13): 0.2, 3B(4): -0.4, LF(4): -0.5	0.2
2018	STL	MLB	23	329	101	.338	-2.5	SS(40): -5.4, 2B(26): -0.8, 3B(24): 0.2	0.2
2019	STL	MLB	24	181	72	.328	0.8	3B(21): -0.1, SS(17): 0.1, RF(12): -0.5	0.0
2020	BOS	MLB	25	45	84	.424	-0.5	LF(7): 0.0, RF(4): 0.4	0.0
2021 FS	BOS	MLB	26	600	90	.305	0.2	SS -1, 2B 0	0.8
2021 DC	BOS	MLB	26	32	90	.305	0.0	SS 0	0.1

Yairo Muñoz, continued

Batted Ball Distribution

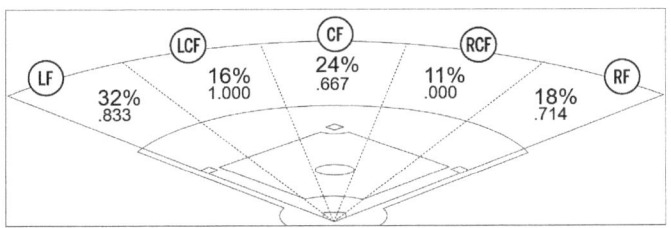

Strike Zone vs LHP

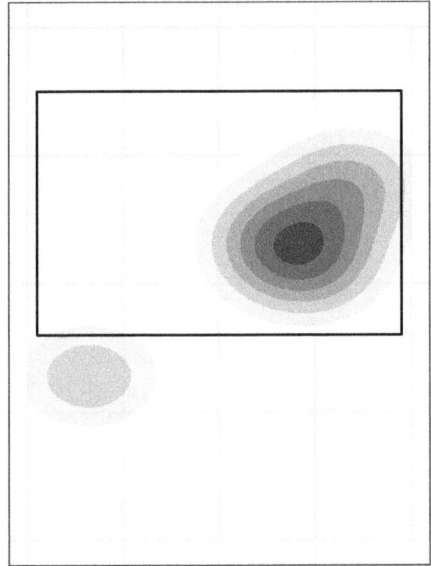

Strike Zone vs RHP

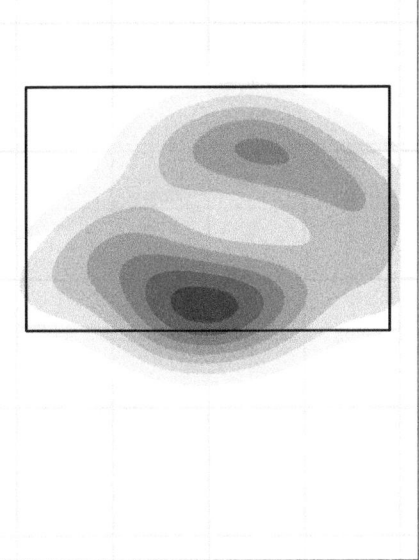

Kevin Plawecki C

Born: 02/26/91   Age: 30   Bats: R   Throws: R
Height: 6'2"   Weight: 208   Origin: Round 1, 2012 Draft (#35 overall)

YEAR	TEAM	LVL	AGE	PA	R	2B	3B	HR	RBI	BB	K	SB	CS	AVG/OBP/SLG
2018	NYM	MLB	27	277	33	13	2	7	30	28	65	0	1	.210/.315/.370
2019	CLE	MLB	28	174	13	10	0	3	17	12	31	0	1	.222/.287/.342
2020	BOS	MLB	29	89	8	5	1	1	17	5	14	1	0	.341/.393/.463
2021 FS	BOS	MLB	30	600	67	27	1	14	65	48	126	1	1	.242/.320/.382
2021 DC	BOS	MLB	30	159	17	7	0	3	17	12	33	0	0	.242/.320/.382

Comparables: Alan Knicely, Terry McGriff, Doug Mirabelli

Relying on BABIP and BABIP alone to assess a player's performance remains the laziest type of "baseball analysis" imaginable, but can you find another way to explain how the lead-footed Plawecki just hit for 100-plus points above his career average?

YEAR	TEAM	P. COUNT	FRM RUNS	BLK RUNS	THRW RUNS	TOT RUNS
2018	NYM	9953	-4.6	2.0	0.0	-2.6
2019	CLE	6790	6.6	2.2	-0.3	8.5
2020	BOS	2969	-3.4	-0.2	0.0	-3.6
2021	BOS	7215	0.0	1.7	0.0	1.8
2021	BOS	7215	0.0	0.0	0.0	0.1

YEAR	TEAM	LVL	AGE	PA	DRC+	BABIP	BRR	FRAA	WARP
2018	NYM	MLB	27	277	92	.257	-1.2	C(71): -2.0, 1B(3): -0.0	0.8
2019	CLE	MLB	28	174	79	.256	-1.3	C(57): 7.8, P(2): -0.0, 1B(1): 0.0	1.1
2020	BOS	MLB	29	89	101	.403	-1.4	C(20): -0.4, 1B(2): 0.0, P(1): -0.0	-0.2
2021 FS	BOS	MLB	30	600	97	.290	-0.8	C 5, 1B 0	2.7
2021 DC	BOS	MLB	30	159	97	.290	-0.2	C 2	0.8

Kevin Plawecki, continued

Batted Ball Distribution

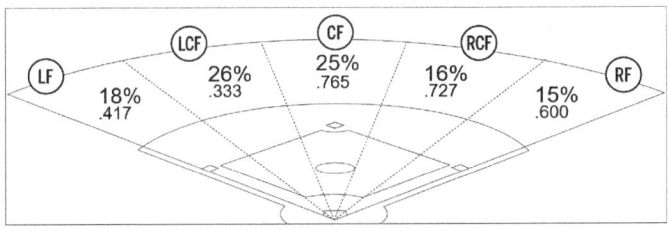

Strike Zone vs LHP   Strike Zone vs RHP

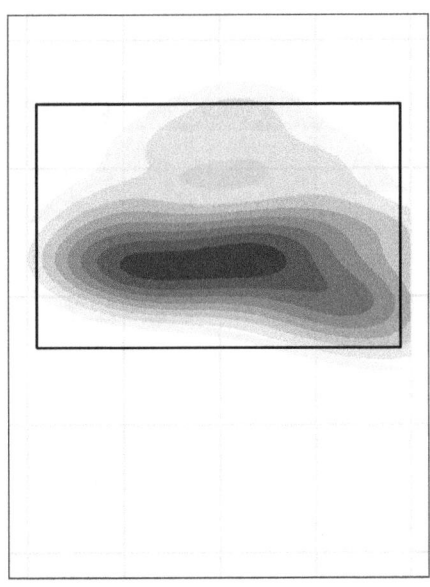

Type	Frequency	Velocity	H Movement	V Movement
● Fastball	100.0%	75 [44]	-6.8 [100]	-29.8 [59]

Hunter Renfroe LF

Born: 01/28/92   Age: 29   Bats: R   Throws: R
Height: 6'1"   Weight: 230   Origin: Round 1, 2013 Draft (#13 overall)

YEAR	TEAM	LVL	AGE	PA	R	2B	3B	HR	RBI	BB	K	SB	CS	AVG/OBP/SLG
2018	ELP	AAA	26	43	6	1	0	2	4	2	10	0	0	.220/.256/.390
2018	SD	MLB	26	441	53	23	1	26	68	30	109	2	1	.248/.302/.504
2019	SD	MLB	27	494	64	19	1	33	64	46	154	5	0	.216/.289/.489
2020	TB	MLB	28	139	18	5	0	8	22	14	37	2	0	.156/.252/.393
2021 FS	BOS	MLB	29	600	77	27	1	31	87	43	173	2	1	.235/.296/.466
2021 DC	BOS	MLB	29	431	55	20	1	22	63	31	124	1	1	.235/.296/.466

Comparables: Yasmany Tomás, Brian Buchanan, Jay Bruce

If Renfroe had the season he had for any team other than the Rays—a year in which he actually improved his plate discipline while maintaining his exit velocity and launch angle—he would probably be on Tampa Bay's wishlist. Instead, they designated him for assignment before Thanksgiving because of their crowded infield and his increasing arbitration bill. Former Rays head honcho Chaim Bloom hopes to turn Tampa's trash into Boston's treasure: he inked Renfroe to a one-year, $3.1 million contract to help man Fenway's cavernous right field.

YEAR	TEAM	LVL	AGE	PA	DRC+	BABIP	BRR	FRAA	WARP
2018	ELP	AAA	26	43	72	.241	-0.1	RF(9): 2.4	0.1
2018	SD	MLB	26	441	110	.271	-1.2	LF(58): -1.3, RF(50): 6.6	2.0
2019	SD	MLB	27	494	98	.239	-2.2	RF(86): 6.5, LF(67): 0.7, CF(4): -0.0	1.6
2020	TB	MLB	28	139	92	.141	-0.6	RF(39): -0.6, 1B(2): 0.1	0.1
2021 FS	BOS	MLB	29	600	107	.281	-0.7	RF 6, 1B 0	2.5
2021 DC	BOS	MLB	29	431	107	.281	-0.5	RF 5	1.7

Hunter Renfroe, continued

Batted Ball Distribution

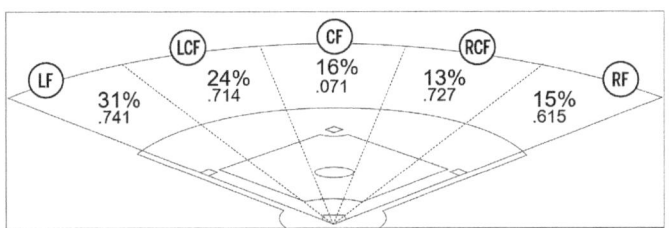

Strike Zone vs LHP   Strike Zone vs RHP

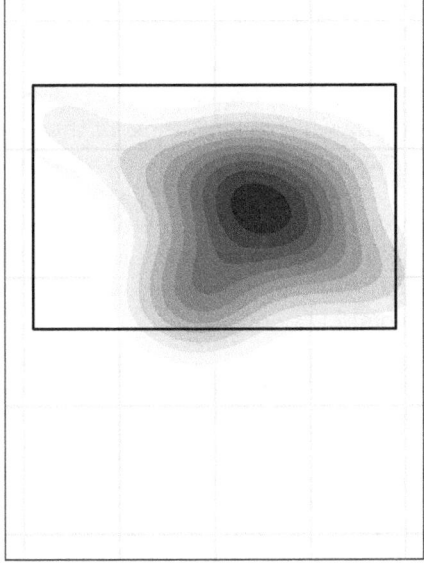

Christian Vázquez C

Born: 08/21/90   Age: 30   Bats: R   Throws: R
Height: 5'9"   Weight: 205   Origin: Round 9, 2008 Draft (#292 overall)

YEAR	TEAM	LVL	AGE	PA	R	2B	3B	HR	RBI	BB	K	SB	CS	AVG/OBP/SLG
2018	BOS	MLB	27	269	24	10	0	3	16	13	41	4	1	.207/.257/.283
2019	BOS	MLB	28	521	66	26	1	23	72	33	101	4	2	.276/.320/.477
2020	BOS	MLB	29	189	22	9	0	7	23	16	43	4	3	.283/.344/.457
2021 FS	BOS	MLB	30	600	66	24	1	17	68	40	134	5	3	.240/.297/.381
2021 DC	BOS	MLB	30	465	51	18	1	13	52	31	104	4	2	.240/.297/.381

Comparables: Jesse Gonder, Cal Neeman, Dan Wilson

YEAR	TEAM	P. COUNT	FRM RUNS	BLK RUNS	THRW RUNS	TOT RUNS
2018	BOS	10488	9.0	0.1	0.1	9.2
2019	BOS	16486	12.3	-5.3	0.8	7.8
2020	BOS	6333	4.2	0.0	-0.1	4.1
2021	BOS	16835	15.3	-1.0	0.3	14.6
2021	BOS	16835	15.3	-0.2	0.3	15.4

When the Red Sox signed Vázquez to a three-year extension before the 2018 season, the prevailing question was ... why? Little about his 2017 performance looked sustainable, and his deal only bought Boston one more year of potential team control via a 2022 option for $7 million. Vázquez initially rewarded Boston's faith by posting a lower DRC+ than Jesus Sucre, but ever since, he's looked like one of the biggest backstop bargains in the game. He followed up his breakout 2019 by finishing as the fifth-best catcher per WARP and CDA while again hitting for the type of power once thought to be well out of his reach. He's still just 30 years old, and as one of the best overall catchers in the game tied to an uber-reasonable contract, one of its best values as well. The Sox could likely fetch a pretty penny for Vazquez should they opt for a dreaded Full Tank, but doing so would prompt a new prevailing inquiry ... isn't Vázquez exactly the type of player you want to build around as you break in new, young pitching?

YEAR	TEAM	LVL	AGE	PA	DRC+	BABIP	BRR	FRAA	WARP
2018	BOS	MLB	27	269	71	.237	-0.4	C(75): 8.3, 3B(2): -0.0	1.2
2019	BOS	MLB	28	521	105	.305	-0.3	C(119): 7.0, 1B(10): 1.0, 3B(4): 0.1	3.5
2020	BOS	MLB	29	189	100	.341	0.0	C(42): 1.0, 2B(1): -0.0	1.2
2021 FS	BOS	MLB	30	600	86	.288	-0.3	C 14, 1B 0	2.7
2021 DC	BOS	MLB	30	465	86	.288	-0.2	C 15	2.6

Christian Vázquez, continued

Batted Ball Distribution

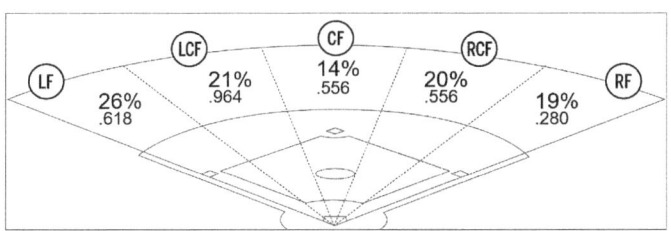

Strike Zone vs LHP   Strike Zone vs RHP

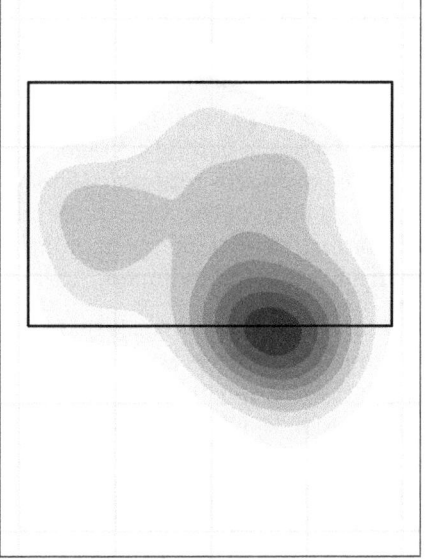

Alex Verdugo CF
Born: 05/15/96   Age: 25   Bats: L   Throws: L
Height: 6'0"   Weight: 192   Origin: Round 2, 2014 Draft (#62 overall)

YEAR	TEAM	LVL	AGE	PA	R	2B	3B	HR	RBI	BB	K	SB	CS	AVG/OBP/SLG
2018	OKC	AAA	22	379	44	19	0	10	44	34	47	8	2	.329/.391/.472
2018	LAD	MLB	22	86	11	6	0	1	4	8	14	0	0	.260/.329/.377
2019	LAD	MLB	23	377	43	22	2	12	44	26	49	4	1	.294/.342/.475
2020	BOS	MLB	24	221	36	16	0	6	15	17	45	4	0	.308/.367/.478
2021 FS	BOS	MLB	25	600	77	28	2	16	62	51	113	1	1	.260/.329/.413
2021 DC	BOS	MLB	25	597	76	28	2	16	62	50	112	1	1	.260/.329/.413

Comparables: Austin Hays, Oscar Mercado, Dave Henderson

It's tough to imagine a young player walking into a more daunting situation than the one Verdugo faced last season. In the blink of a salary dump, he went from a part-time player on a juggernaut to the focal point of the dumpster fire that was the 2020 Red Sox. Just 24 years old and with less than a full season of playing time under his belt, Verdugo strolled into Fenway Park to man the same spot—right field—that a franchise icon had been evicted from just months before. Many would've buckled under the weight of the expectations, but Verdugo passed his stress test with flying colors.

Despite the gaze of an irate fanbase and the lingering effects of a back injury that ended his 2019 campaign, Verdugo excelled in Boston from day one. He paced the Sox in batting average, OBP and doubles while placing second in WARP en route to a 12th-place finish in AL MVP voting. He played solid defense across all three outfield spots, seemed fully engaged in all aspects of the game, and brought a high-energy approach to the team. He was as good, if not better, than anyone could've hoped.

The problem, of course, is that while Verdugo was establishing himself in Boston, Mookie Betts was helping the Dodgers win the World Series. It's an unfair comparison, but one that will plague Verdugo throughout his Red Sox career. There's nothing he can do about that, but in year one, Verdugo excelled at everything he could control, showing the talent and health needed to thrive despite the circumstances. He can't make the Betts trade a *good* one for Boston, but he can cement himself as an integral part of the next good Red Sox team. He looks well on his way to doing so.

YEAR	TEAM	LVL	AGE	PA	DRC+	BABIP	BRR	FRAA	WARP
2018	OKC	AAA	22	379	129	.359	-0.5	CF(45): 2.0, RF(31): 2.4, LF(13): -0.4	2.2
2018	LAD	MLB	22	86	85	.306	1.5	RF(16): -0.1, LF(12): 0.2, CF(8): -1.0	0.1
2019	LAD	MLB	23	377	102	.309	1.4	CF(61): -1.2, RF(25): 1.2, LF(22): 2.0	1.7
2020	BOS	MLB	24	221	101	.371	1.7	RF(31): -2.2, LF(22): 0.7, CF(1): -0.1	0.9
2021 FS	BOS	MLB	25	600	103	.303	-0.7	CF 2, RF 1	2.1
2021 DC	BOS	MLB	25	597	103	.303	-0.7	CF 2, RF 1	2.2

Batted Ball Distribution

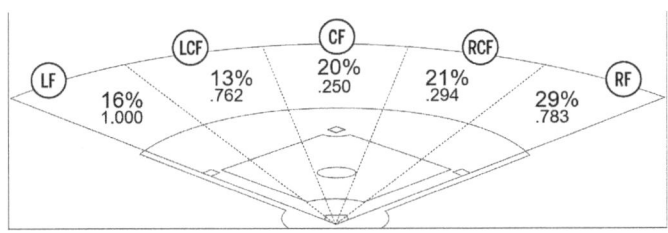

Strike Zone vs LHP   **Strike Zone vs RHP**

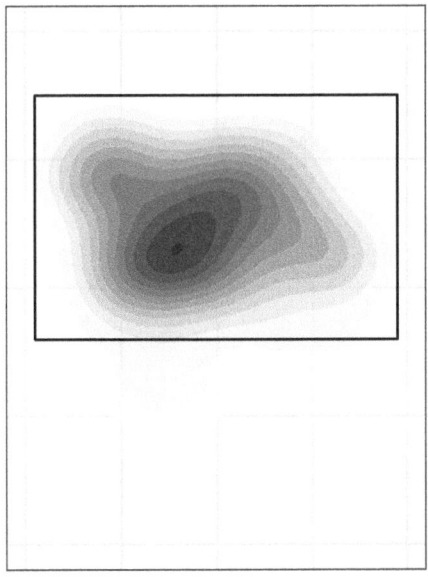

Matt Andriese RHP

Born: 08/28/89   Age: 31   Bats: R   Throws: R
Height: 6'2"   Weight: 215   Origin: Round 3, 2011 Draft (#112 overall)

YEAR	TEAM	LVL	AGE	W	L	SV	G	GS	IP	H	HR	BB/9	K/9	K	GB%	BABIP
2018	TB	MLB	28	3	4	0	27	4	59^2	55	7	2.7	8.9	59	49.4%	.293
2018	ARI	MLB	28	0	3	0	14	1	19	29	8	3.3	9.0	19	42.9%	.382
2019	ARI	MLB	29	5	5	1	54	0	70^2	72	8	3.4	10.1	79	49.5%	.335
2020	LAA	MLB	30	2	4	2	16	1	32	21	5	3.1	9.3	33	45.7%	.211
2021 FS	BOS	MLB	31	10	7	0	26	26	150	135	20	2.8	9.2	152	46.2%	.289
2021 DC	BOS	MLB	31	7	5	0	45	9	87.7	79	11	2.8	9.2	89	46.2%	.289

Comparables: Erasmo Ramírez, Alex Colomé, Trevor May

It is not, generally, considered good practice for a front office to acquire a relief pitcher coming off a season head and shoulders beyond their previous best effort. It's basically the Colorado Rockies' entire organizational philosophy, and things aren't going great up there. Predictably, Andriese regressed from his career-best 2019 DRA, and failed to break into an Angels rotation whose only defense against rogue entrants is an ADT security sign so faded it's more baby than blue. Still, a reliable multi-inning reliever is hard to come by, and Andriese, for everything else he lacks, is nothing if not reliable.

YEAR	TEAM	LVL	AGE	WHIP	ERA	DRA-	WARP	MPH	FB%	WHF	CSP
2018	TB	MLB	28	1.22	4.07	109	0.1	93.8	46.1%	25.7%	
2018	ARI	MLB	28	1.89	9.00	116	0.0	93.8	48.9%	25.9%	
2019	ARI	MLB	29	1.40	4.71	74	1.3	94.2	50.5%	25.4%	
2020	LAA	MLB	30	1.00	4.50	90	0.5	93.5	43.2%	22.6%	
2021 FS	BOS	MLB	31	1.22	3.45	87	2.6	93.9	47.4%	24.7%	48.4%
2021 DC	BOS	MLB	31	1.22	3.45	87	1.2	93.9	47.4%	24.7%	48.4%

Matt Andriese, continued

Pitch Shape vs LHH

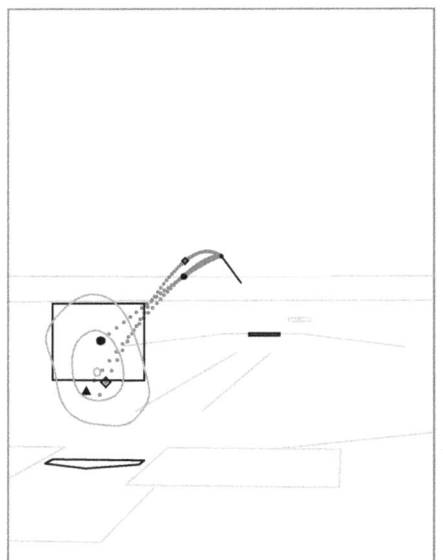

Pitch Shape vs RHH

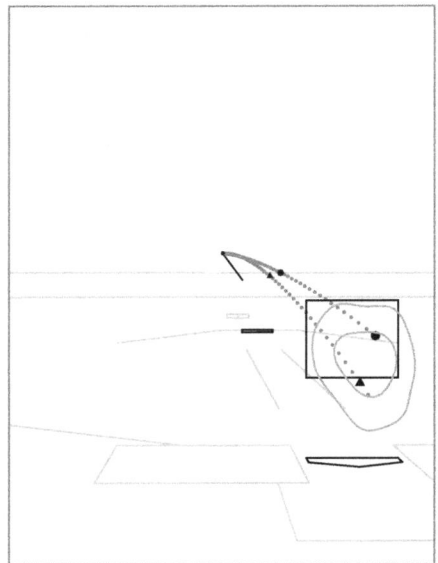

Type	Frequency	Velocity	H Movement	V Movement
● Fastball	36.8%	92 [98]	-7.1 [98]	-14.1 [103]
☐ Sinker	6.4%	90.8 [92]	-14.2 [92]	-22.1 [95]
+ Cutter	6.4%	85.9 [85]	2.1 [102]	-30 [77]
▲ Changeup	38.6%	86 [103]	-3.7 [143]	-31.6 [89]
◇ Curveball	11.8%	80.1 [106]	4.8 [89]	-50.2 [96]

Matt Barnes RHP
Born: 06/17/90 Age: 31 Bats: R Throws: R
Height: 6'4" Weight: 208 Origin: Round 1, 2011 Draft (#19 overall)

YEAR	TEAM	LVL	AGE	W	L	SV	G	GS	IP	H	HR	BB/9	K/9	K	GB%	BABIP
2018	BOS	MLB	28	6	4	0	62	0	61^2	47	5	4.5	14.0	96	51.5%	.321
2019	BOS	MLB	29	5	4	4	70	0	64^1	51	8	5.3	15.4	110	47.8%	.341
2020	BOS	MLB	30	1	3	9	24	0	23	18	4	5.5	12.1	31	45.5%	.280
2021 FS	BOS	MLB	31	2	2	26	57	0	50	39	5	4.8	12.2	67	46.5%	.301
2021 DC	BOS	MLB	31	3	2	26	61	0	61	48	6	4.8	12.2	83	46.5%	.301

Comparables: Alex Colomé, Neil Ramírez, Tommy Kahnle

Barnes' high-strikeout, high-walk, high-wire act works reasonably well when, as in 2019, he's whiffing among the highest percentage of batters in all of baseball. But one of the biggest problems with such a dangerous approach is how little margin it leaves for error. Barnes still missed a ton of bats in 2020, but an eight percentage point drop in K% is tough to stomach when you're walking every seventh batter you face—even when said drop still leaves your K% in the 30s. Barnes has performed fairly consistently over the past several seasons, and there's no reason to overreact to a 24-game sample. That being said, his recent struggles illustrate that while he may seem capable of breaking into the game's upper echelon of relievers, he's arguably more prone to sliding back into its murky middle tier of firemen.

YEAR	TEAM	LVL	AGE	WHIP	ERA	DRA-	WARP	MPH	FB%	WHF	CSP
2018	BOS	MLB	28	1.26	3.65	49	1.9	98.5	54.8%	36.4%	
2019	BOS	MLB	29	1.38	3.78	56	1.8	98.1	47.1%	36.3%	
2020	BOS	MLB	30	1.39	4.30	81	0.4	97.1	54.1%	28.6%	
2021 FS	BOS	MLB	31	1.32	3.42	83	0.7	97.9	50.7%	34.2%	40.8%
2021 DC	BOS	MLB	31	1.32	3.42	83	0.9	97.9	50.7%	34.2%	40.8%

Matt Barnes, continued

Pitch Shape vs LHH

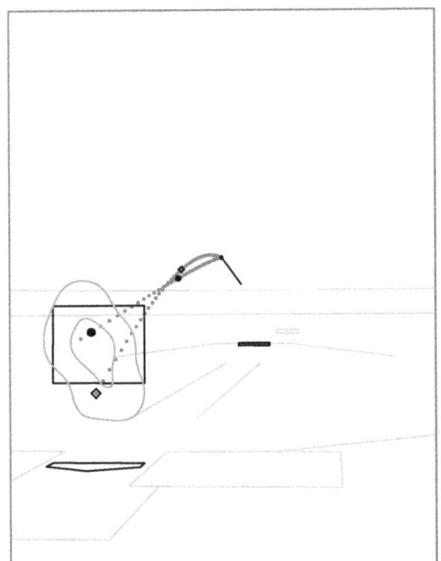

Pitch Shape vs RHH

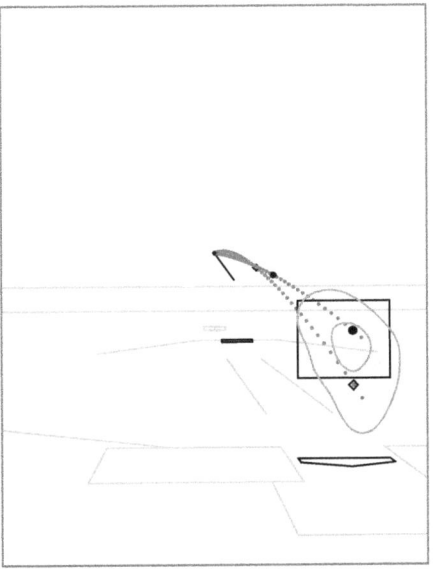

Type	Frequency	Velocity	H Movement	V Movement
● Fastball	53.6%	95.7 [110]	-9.8 [85]	-12 [109]
◇ Curveball	42.7%	84.8 [124]	3.2 [82]	-43.6 [111]

Ryan Brasier RHP

Born: 08/26/87 Age: 33 Bats: R Throws: R
Height: 6'0" Weight: 227 Origin: Round 6, 2007 Draft (#208 overall)

YEAR	TEAM	LVL	AGE	W	L	SV	G	GS	IP	H	HR	BB/9	K/9	K	GB%	BABIP
2018	WOR	AAA	30	2	5	13	34	0	40^1	29	1	1.8	8.9	40	38.2%	.289
2018	BOS	MLB	30	2	0	0	34	0	33^2	19	2	1.9	7.8	29	42.0%	.200
2019	WOR	AAA	31	2	0	0	10	0	9^1	6	1	1.0	12.5	13	45.0%	.263
2019	BOS	MLB	31	2	4	7	62	0	55^2	51	9	3.4	9.7	60	32.1%	.284
2020	BOS	MLB	32	1	0	0	25	1	25	24	2	4.0	10.8	30	37.7%	.328
2021 FS	BOS	MLB	33	2	2	3	57	0	50	43	7	3.1	9.7	54	37.5%	.284
2021 DC	BOS	MLB	33	3	3	3	61	0	61	53	9	3.1	9.7	66	37.5%	.284

Comparables: Ryan Tepera, Cory Gearrin, Bryan Shaw

It's never a good sign when one of your most-used relievers finishes a season with more apologies for racially insensitive tweets than saves, but Brasier proved up to that ignominious task. As a pitcher, Brasier found middle ground between his terrific 2018 and his abysmal 2019, settling in as a league-average reliever who misses bats but who also misses the plate too much to truly shine. As a (re)tweeter, he made headlines for Milkshake Duck-ing himself just hours after the Red Sox and Blue Jays agreed to postpone their game in an act of protest against racism and police brutality. It was awfully fun at the time to watch Brasier bark at Gary Sánchez in the 2018 postseason, but now it seems as though the less we hear from Brasier on *or* off the mound, the better.

YEAR	TEAM	LVL	AGE	WHIP	ERA	DRA-	WARP	MPH	FB%	WHF	CSP
2018	WOR	AAA	30	0.92	1.34	65	0.9				
2018	BOS	MLB	30	0.77	1.60	79	0.5	98.2	62.6%	31.0%	
2019	WOR	AAA	31	0.75	0.96	46	0.4				
2019	BOS	MLB	31	1.29	4.85	110	0.0	97.5	59.2%	31.2%	
2020	BOS	MLB	32	1.40	3.96	83	0.4	97.6	62.0%	34.1%	
2021 FS	BOS	MLB	33	1.22	3.52	89	0.6	97.6	60.7%	32.2%	45.5%
2021 DC	BOS	MLB	33	1.22	3.52	89	0.7	97.6	60.7%	32.2%	45.5%

Ryan Brasier, continued

Pitch Shape vs LHH

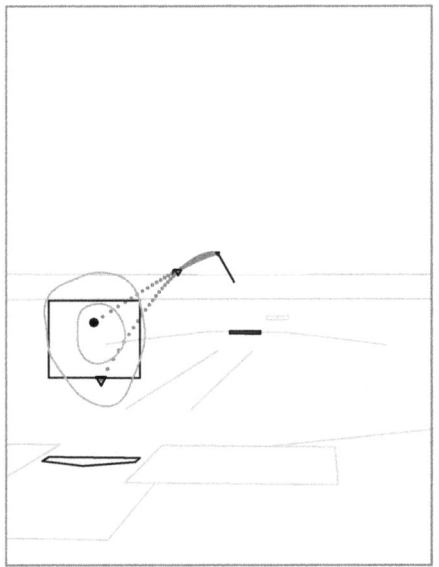

Pitch Shape vs RHH

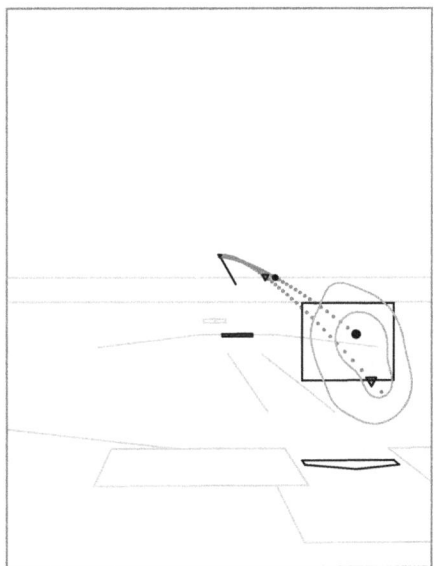

Type	Frequency	Velocity	H Movement	V Movement
● Fastball	58.4%	96.4 [112]	-6.6 [100]	-11.9 [109]
□ Sinker	3.0%	95.3 [115]	-14.2 [92]	-16.3 [114]
▲ Changeup	4.9%	87.6 [110]	-12.6 [96]	-26.9 [102]
▽ Slider	32.7%	86.3 [111]	5.7 [102]	-31.6 [106]

Colten Brewer RHP

Born: 10/29/92 Age: 28 Bats: R Throws: R
Height: 6'4" Weight: 222 Origin: Round 4, 2011 Draft (#122 overall)

YEAR	TEAM	LVL	AGE	W	L	SV	G	GS	IP	H	HR	BB/9	K/9	K	GB%	BABIP
2018	ELP	AAA	25	3	4	3	37	0	48	40	3	2.8	11.8	63	54.8%	.333
2018	SD	MLB	25	1	0	0	11	0	9^2	15	0	6.5	9.3	10	50.0%	.469
2019	WOR	AAA	26	2	3	0	9	0	11	14	2	5.7	8.2	10	54.1%	.353
2019	BOS	MLB	26	1	2	0	58	0	54^2	59	6	5.6	8.6	52	52.1%	.335
2020	BOS	MLB	27	0	3	0	11	4	25^2	31	6	4.9	8.8	25	51.2%	.329
2021 FS	BOS	MLB	28	2	2	0	57	0	50	47	5	4.9	8.9	49	51.2%	.304
2021 DC	BOS	MLB	28	2	2	0	54	0	36.3	35	4	4.9	8.9	36	51.2%	.304

Comparables: Dovydas Neverauskas, Yacksel Ríos, Michael Feliz

The Red Sox have improved the beer selection at Fenway Park in recent years but fell flat when importing Brewer, who gave up nearly a homer per four innings pitched. He does not belong on the 40-man roster of a team that is trying to win games, yet just finished third among Red Sox relievers in innings pitched.

YEAR	TEAM	LVL	AGE	WHIP	ERA	DRA-	WARP	MPH	FB%	WHF	CSP
2018	ELP	AAA	25	1.15	3.75	52	1.5				
2018	SD	MLB	25	2.28	5.59	60	0.2	95.0	68.0%	29.6%	
2019	WOR	AAA	26	1.91	4.91	134	0.0				
2019	BOS	MLB	26	1.70	4.12	106	0.1	95.4	44.5%	27.3%	
2020	BOS	MLB	27	1.75	5.61	104	0.2	95.3	47.2%	22.6%	
2021 FS	BOS	MLB	28	1.51	4.53	104	0.1	95.3	46.9%	25.5%	44.1%
2021 DC	BOS	MLB	28	1.51	4.53	104	0.1	95.3	46.9%	25.5%	44.1%

Colten Brewer, continued

Pitch Shape vs LHH

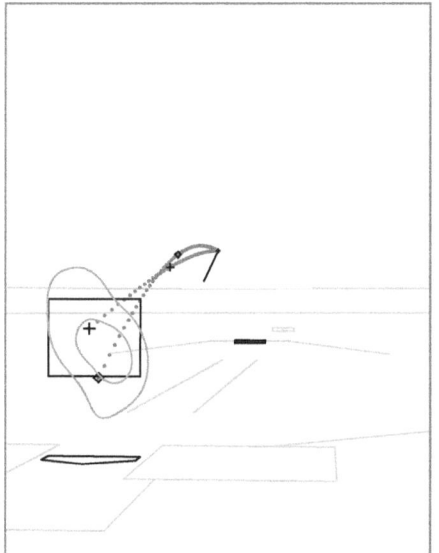

Pitch Shape vs RHH

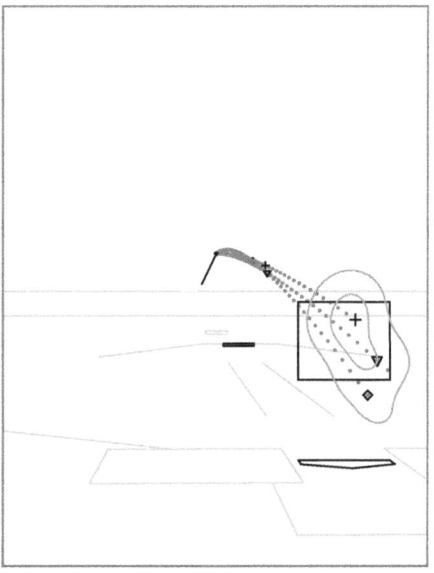

Type	Frequency	Velocity	H Movement	V Movement
+ Cutter	45.1%	93.8 [135]	1.6 [98]	-18.4 [123]
▽ Slider	19.6%	89 [123]	4.3 [96]	-26.1 [122]
◇ Curveball	32.8%	80.9 [109]	9.6 [108]	-51.6 [93]

Boston Red Sox 2021

Austin Brice RHP
Born: 06/19/92   Age: 29   Bats: R   Throws: R
Height: 6'4"   Weight: 238   Origin: Round 9, 2010 Draft (#287 overall)

YEAR	TEAM	LVL	AGE	W	L	SV	G	GS	IP	H	HR	BB/9	K/9	K	GB%	BABIP
2018	LOU	AAA	26	3	1	1	17	0	23¹	18	2	2.7	9.3	24	35.7%	.296
2018	CIN	MLB	26	2	3	0	33	0	37¹	39	9	3.1	7.7	32	51.8%	.288
2019	MIA	MLB	27	1	0	0	36	0	44²	37	7	3.6	9.3	46	42.2%	.248
2020	BOS	MLB	28	1	0	0	21	1	19²	17	3	5.9	11.4	25	42.6%	.318
2021 FS	BOS	MLB	29	2	2	0	57	0	50	45	6	3.8	9.9	54	42.1%	.299
2021 DC	BOS	MLB	29	2	2	0	54	0	48.7	44	6	3.8	9.9	53	42.1%	.299

Comparables: Hansel Robles, Kevin McCarthy, Bobby Parnell

Can you name which of these Brice facts is not true?

A) He is the first player born in Hong Kong to reach the majors

B) He was acquired by the Red Sox for a man named "Angeudis Santos"

C) He just posted the 45th highest BB/9 rate of any pitcher who threw at least 10 IP

D) He was once a part of the Reds' Luis Castillo trade

The answer is C—Brice's walk rate was *43rd* highest.

YEAR	TEAM	LVL	AGE	WHIP	ERA	DRA-	WARP	MPH	FB%	WHF	CSP
2018	LOU	AAA	26	1.07	2.31	87	0.2				
2018	CIN	MLB	26	1.39	5.79	128	-0.4	95.4	68.4%	21.7%	
2019	MIA	MLB	27	1.23	3.43	92	0.4	94.6	51.0%	26.7%	
2020	BOS	MLB	28	1.53	5.95	89	0.3	94.9	61.8%	34.4%	
2021 FS	BOS	MLB	29	1.33	4.09	97	0.3	94.9	57.9%	28.3%	46.9%
2021 DC	BOS	MLB	29	1.33	4.09	97	0.3	94.9	57.9%	28.3%	46.9%

Austin Brice, continued

Pitch Shape vs LHH

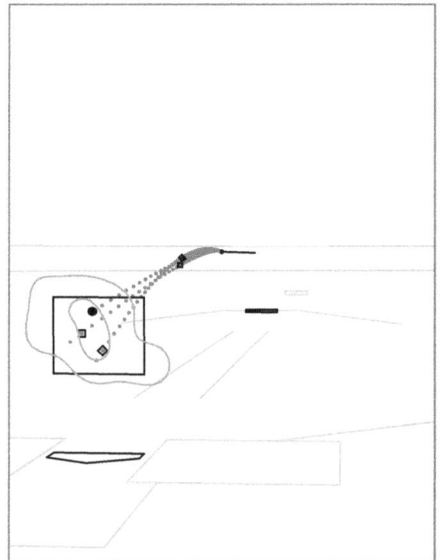

Pitch Shape vs RHH

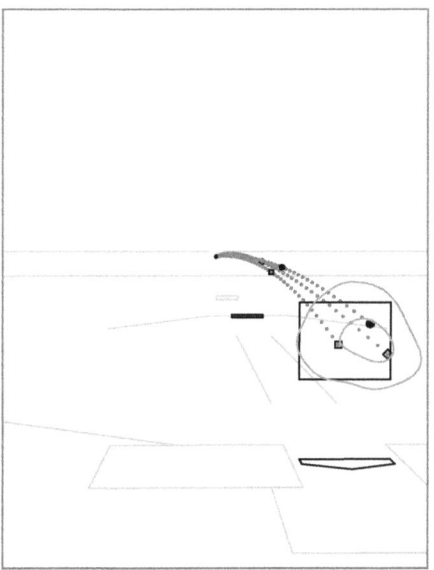

Type	Frequency	Velocity	H Movement	V Movement
● Fastball	28.4%	94.1 [105]	-14 [65]	-20.7 [84]
☐ Sinker	33.4%	93.7 [106]	-15.5 [82]	-25.6 [84]
◇ Curveball	37.3%	81.9 [113]	7.1 [98]	-37 [125]

Nathan Eovaldi   RHP

Born: 02/13/90 Age: 31 Bats: R Throws: R
Height: 6'2"   Weight: 217   Origin: Round 11, 2008 Draft (#337 overall)

YEAR	TEAM	LVL	AGE	W	L	SV	G	GS	IP	H	HR	BB/9	K/9	K	GB%	BABIP
2018	CHA	HI-A	28	0	0	0	3	3	6	6	2	0.0	10.5	7	47.1%	.267
2018	BOS	MLB	28	3	3	0	12	11	54	57	3	2.0	8.0	48	45.6%	.327
2018	TB	MLB	28	3	4	0	10	10	57	48	11	1.3	8.4	53	46.9%	.245
2019	BOS	MLB	29	2	1	0	23	12	67^2	72	16	4.7	9.3	70	44.3%	.316
2020	BOS	MLB	30	4	2	0	9	9	48^1	51	8	1.3	9.7	52	49.3%	.339
2021 FS	BOS	MLB	31	10	7	0	26	26	150	137	18	2.7	9.2	153	47.2%	.296
2021 DC	BOS	MLB	31	8	6	0	24	22	124.7	114	15	2.7	9.2	127	47.2%	.296

Comparables: Jake Odorizzi, Rick Porcello, Anthony DeSclafani

Eovaldi picked a bad time to have a good season. When the quasi-competitive Sox needed Eovaldi most in 2019 he could not answer the bell thanks to his oft-troublesome right elbow and an utter lack of command. Yet when the 2020 Red Sox were in Full Tank Mode, the good Eovaldi showed up once more, posting the best strikeout rate and second-best DRA of his career while pacing the Sox in PWARP. Of course no Eovaldi season is complete without a trip to the IL, and he obliged this time around with a strained calf. All things considered, that counts as good news on the Eovaldi injury front, especially since the Sox still owe their 2018 postseason hero $34 million over the next two seasons.

YEAR	TEAM	LVL	AGE	WHIP	ERA	DRA-	WARP	MPH	FB%	WHF	CSP
2018	CHA	HI-A	28	1.00	4.50	71	0.1				
2018	BOS	MLB	28	1.28	3.33	73	1.3	99.8	38.1%	21.3%	
2018	TB	MLB	28	0.98	4.26	71	1.4	98.7	41.6%	22.8%	
2019	BOS	MLB	29	1.58	5.99	130	-0.5	99.7	43.6%	26.3%	
2020	BOS	MLB	30	1.20	3.72	80	1.0	99.5	37.7%	28.1%	
2021 FS	BOS	MLB	31	1.22	3.37	84	2.7	99.5	40.6%	25.8%	49.3%
2021 DC	BOS	MLB	31	1.22	3.37	84	2.2	99.5	40.6%	25.8%	49.3%

Nathan Eovaldi, continued

Pitch Shape vs LHH

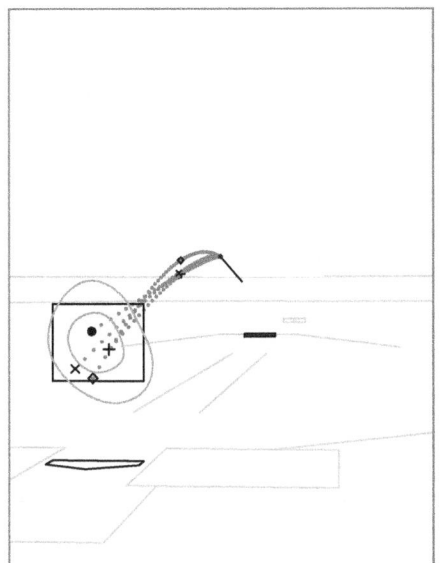

Pitch Shape vs RHH

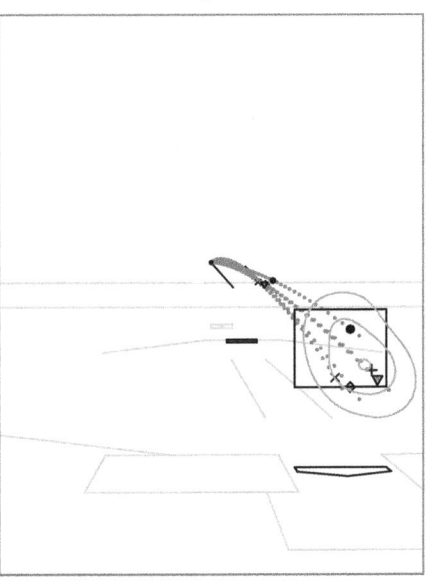

Type	Frequency	Velocity	H Movement	V Movement
● Fastball	37.7%	97.6 [116]	-9.7 [86]	-13.5 [105]
+ Cutter	21.5%	92.3 [125]	1.4 [97]	-22.7 [106]
✕ Splitter	14.2%	88.1 [113]	-8.2 [99]	-30.1 [98]
▽ Slider	9.5%	89.3 [124]	3.8 [94]	-27.3 [119]
◇ Curveball	17.1%	79.8 [105]	7.7 [100]	-45.7 [106]

Zack Godley RHP

Born: 04/21/90   Age: 31   Bats: R   Throws: R
Height: 6'3"   Weight: 250   Origin: Round 10, 2013 Draft (#288 overall)

YEAR	TEAM	LVL	AGE	W	L	SV	G	GS	IP	H	HR	BB/9	K/9	K	GB%	BABIP
2018	ARI	MLB	28	15	11	0	33	32	178^1	177	16	4.1	9.3	185	47.8%	.329
2019	ARI	MLB	29	3	5	2	27	9	76	81	12	4.1	6.9	58	42.9%	.307
2019	TOR	MLB	29	1	0	0	6	0	16	15	2	3.9	6.8	12	42.9%	.277
2020	BOS	MLB	30	0	4	0	8	7	28^2	42	9	4.4	8.8	28	40.8%	.371
2021 FS	BOS	MLB	31	2	3	0	57	0	50	50	7	4.1	8.3	46	44.2%	.304

Comparables: Matt Andriese, Anthony DeSclafani, Jake Odorizzi

A former feel-good story, Godley added injury to insulting performance by ending the year on the IL with a right flexor strain. In total, he gave us the ugliest Godley experience in New England since the Salem Witch Trials.

YEAR	TEAM	LVL	AGE	WHIP	ERA	DRA-	WARP	MPH	FB%	WHF	CSP
2018	ARI	MLB	28	1.45	4.74	106	1.1	91.5	54.3%	27.8%	
2019	ARI	MLB	29	1.53	6.39	137	-1.0	91.7	49.0%	23.7%	
2019	TOR	MLB	29	1.38	3.94	107	0.0	91.5	65.3%	28.4%	
2020	BOS	MLB	30	1.95	8.16	127	-0.2	91.1	51.7%	25.6%	
2021 FS	BOS	MLB	31	1.47	4.81	110	-0.1	91.5	52.7%	26.0%	43.6%

Zack Godley, continued

Pitch Shape vs LHH

Pitch Shape vs RHH

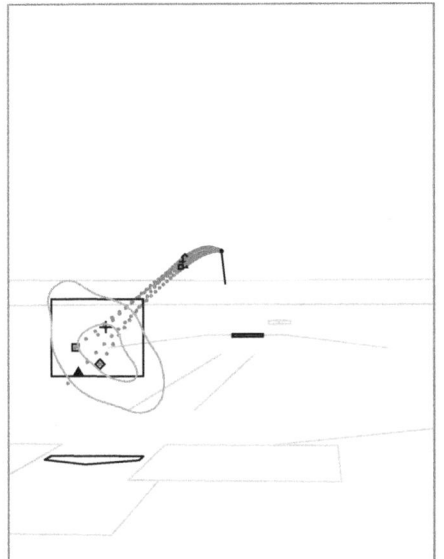 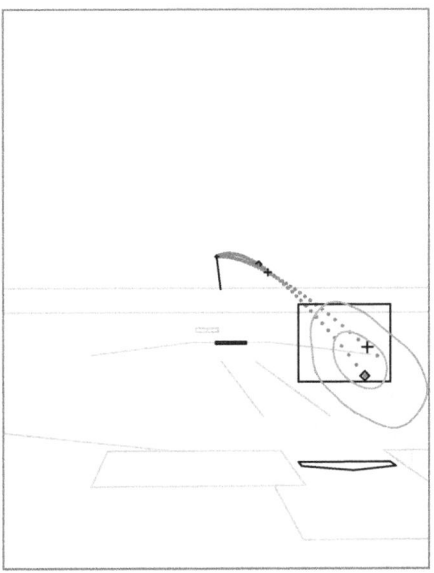

Type	Frequency	Velocity	H Movement	V Movement
☐ Sinker	8.3%	89.6 [86]	-12.7 [103]	-25.5 [84]
+ Cutter	40.7%	88.9 [103]	-0.6 [84]	-23.4 [103]
▲ Changeup	10.1%	83.3 [93]	-11.8 [100]	-34.5 [81]
◇ Curveball	38.2%	82.2 [114]	1.9 [77]	-42.6 [113]

Darwinzon Hernandez   LHP
Born: 12/17/96   Age: 24   Bats: L   Throws: L
Height: 6'2"   Weight: 255   Origin: International Free Agent, 2013

YEAR	TEAM	LVL	AGE	W	L	SV	G	GS	IP	H	HR	BB/9	K/9	K	GB%	BABIP
2018	SAL	HI-A	21	9	5	0	23	23	101	80	1	5.3	11.0	124	43.6%	.331
2018	POR	AA	21	0	0	0	5	0	6	6	0	9.0	15.0	10	35.7%	.429
2019	POR	AA	22	1	4	0	10	9	40¹	33	2	7.1	13.2	59	35.8%	.341
2019	WOR	AAA	22	1	2	0	7	3	17	10	2	8.5	10.6	20	35.1%	.229
2019	BOS	MLB	22	0	1	0	29	1	30¹	27	1	7.7	16.9	57	42.6%	.441
2020	BOS	MLB	23	1	0	0	7	0	8¹	5	0	8.6	14.0	13	50.0%	.278
2021 FS	BOS	MLB	24	2	3	0	57	0	50	42	5	7.7	11.9	66	40.6%	.313
2021 DC	BOS	MLB	24	2	2	0	48	0	36.3	30	3	7.7	11.9	48	40.6%	.313

Comparables: Touki Toussaint, José Castillo, Patrick Sandoval

It was a tough year for Darwinism all around, and that extended to Hernandez. In theory, Boston's decision to punt on the 2020 season should've afforded the fireballing lefty a chance to prove he belonged in a big-league rotation. Instead, Hernandez missed most of the year following a bout with COVID-19, unable to join the active roster until late August. In the few games in which he played, Hernandez looked the same as ever: utterly overpowering and ludicrously wild. His upside is such that he deserves to be a part of Boston's plans moving forward, but at present it's still tough to trust him with much beyond medium-leverage work.

YEAR	TEAM	LVL	AGE	WHIP	ERA	DRA-	WARP	MPH	FB%	WHF	CSP
2018	SAL	HI-A	21	1.39	3.56	105	0.5				
2018	POR	AA	21	2.00	3.00	50	0.2				
2019	POR	AA	22	1.61	5.13	103	-0.1				
2019	WOR	AAA	22	1.53	4.76	96	0.3				
2019	BOS	MLB	22	1.75	4.45	62	0.8	97.7	74.4%	35.5%	
2020	BOS	MLB	23	1.56	2.16	86	0.1	96.4	72.7%	27.5%	
2021 FS	BOS	MLB	24	1.70	5.21	111	-0.1	97.4	73.9%	33.2%	47.6%
2021 DC	BOS	MLB	24	1.70	5.21	111	0.0	97.4	73.9%	33.2%	47.6%

Darwinzon Hernandez, continued

Pitch Shape vs LHH

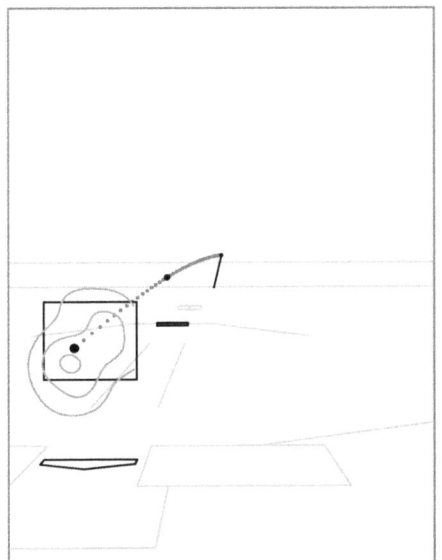

Pitch Shape vs RHH

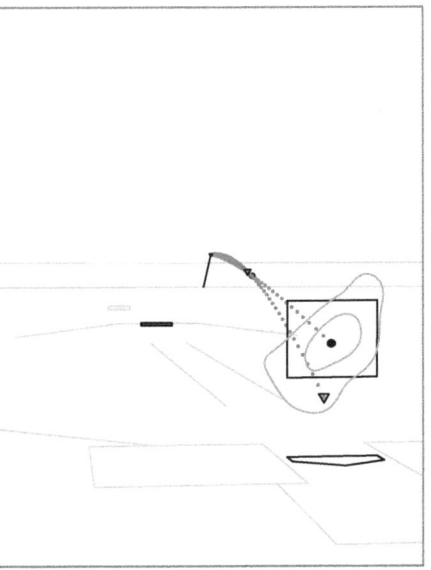

Type	Frequency	Velocity	H Movement	V Movement
● Fastball	72.7%	94.3 [106]	2.1 [122]	-16.6 [96]
▽ Slider	25.0%	83.4 [97]	-6.8 [106]	-36.8 [91]

Tanner Houck RHP

Born: 06/29/96   Age: 25   Bats: R   Throws: R
Height: 6'5"   Weight: 230   Origin: Round 1, 2017 Draft (#24 overall)

YEAR	TEAM	LVL	AGE	W	L	SV	G	GS	IP	H	HR	BB/9	K/9	K	GB%	BABIP
2018	SAL	HI-A	22	7	11	0	23	23	119	110	11	4.5	8.4	111	49.3%	.299
2019	POR	AA	23	8	6	0	17	15	82²	86	4	3.5	8.7	80	48.5%	.346
2019	WOR	AAA	23	0	0	1	16	2	25	19	3	5.0	9.7	27	43.3%	.258
2020	BOS	MLB	24	3	0	0	3	3	17	6	1	4.8	11.1	21	46.9%	.161
2021 FS	BOS	MLB	25	9	9	0	26	26	150	138	19	5.2	9.3	154	45.4%	.297
2021 DC	BOS	MLB	25	7	7	0	25	22	120	111	15	5.2	9.3	124	45.4%	.297

Comparables: Jayson Aquino, Keury Mella, Cal Quantrill

If someone forces you at gunpoint to rewatch part of the 2020 Red Sox season, pick Houck's three starts. Boston's 2017 first-rounder dazzled in his major league cameo, leaning on a wipeout slider, two types of fastball and a funky delivery to pile up the Ks while allowing just one earned run. Houck isn't a finished product, but per the inimitable Alex Speier, it's Houck's athleticism and openness to change that've helped him evolve into a potential rotation piece. The Sox have asked him to tweak his delivery, refine his approach against lefties, bounce between roles and develop a two-seamer he can use up in the zone. The early results haven't always been pretty, but Houck has stuck with it, and he's routinely bounced back from tough starts at various levels. Boston hasn't developed a good, homegrown starter in a long while, which is why Houck's three-game sample led to desperate comps like "Corey Kluber-lite" or "right-handed Chris Sale." In truth, the Sox should be overjoyed if Houck can stick as a No. 3/4 starter with upside. Anything more than that is house money, though given Houck's proven ability to adjust, we can't put it past him.

YEAR	TEAM	LVL	AGE	WHIP	ERA	DRA-	WARP	MPH	FB%	WHF	CSP
2018	SAL	HI-A	22	1.43	4.24	119	-0.4				
2019	POR	AA	23	1.43	4.25	112	-0.5				
2019	WOR	AAA	23	1.32	3.24	72	0.7				
2020	BOS	MLB	24	0.88	0.53	85	0.3	95.1	62.3%	27.1%	
2021 FS	BOS	MLB	25	1.50	4.71	108	0.7	95.1	62.3%	27.1%	42.8%
2021 DC	BOS	MLB	25	1.50	4.71	108	0.6	95.1	62.3%	27.1%	42.8%

Tanner Houck, continued

Pitch Shape vs LHH

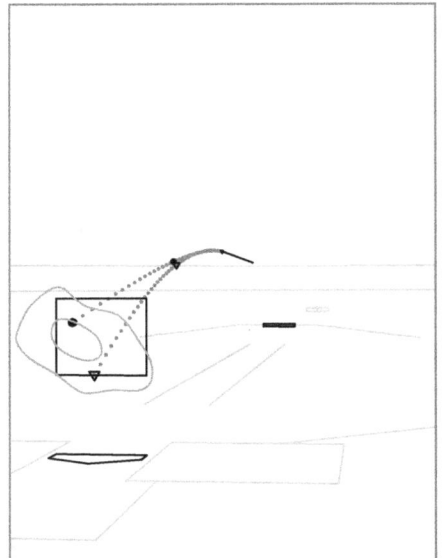

Pitch Shape vs RHH

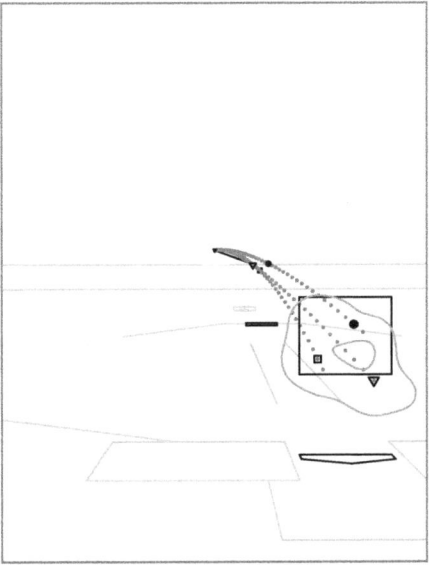

Type	Frequency	Velocity	H Movement	V Movement
● Fastball	35.5%	92.9 [101]	-4.8 [109]	-21.4 [83]
□ Sinker	26.8%	91.2 [94]	-13.7 [96]	-28.2 [75]
▽ Slider	35.5%	82.4 [93]	12.4 [127]	-36.5 [92]

Robinson Leyer RHP

Born: 03/13/93 Age: 28 Bats: R Throws: R
Height: 6'2" Weight: 185 Origin: International Free Agent, 2011

YEAR	TEAM	LVL	AGE	W	L	SV	G	GS	IP	H	HR	BB/9	K/9	K	GB%	BABIP
2018	PNS	AA	25	6	3	2	42	0	59	43	4	4.3	9.9	65	39.0%	.277
2019	POR	AA	26	0	1	0	15	1	23^2	13	0	6.5	11.4	30	33.3%	.255
2019	ARK	AA	26	1	0	1	9	0	10^1	19	0	6.1	9.6	11	38.5%	.487
2019	TAC	AAA	26	1	1	0	13	0	19^2	20	3	5.0	12.4	27	32.7%	.370
2020	BOS	MLB	27	0	0	0	6	1	4^2	12	3	15.4	17.4	9	35.3%	.643
2021 FS	*BOS*	*MLB*	*28*	*2*	*3*	*0*	*57*	*0*	*50*	*46*	*7*	*5.5*	*9.9*	*54*	*35.3%*	*.298*

Comparables: Tayler Scott, Josh Ravin, Brandon Brennan

Good luck finding a more absurd stat line than the one just posted by the electric, eclectic Leyer; his strikeout rate could drive, his walk rate should be studying for the PSATs and his ERA could legally drink.

YEAR	TEAM	LVL	AGE	WHIP	ERA	DRA-	WARP	MPH	FB%	WHF	CSP
2018	PNS	AA	25	1.20	2.59	79	0.8				
2019	POR	AA	26	1.27	2.66	87	0.1				
2019	ARK	AA	26	2.52	8.71	172	-0.5				
2019	TAC	AAA	26	1.58	4.58	94	0.3				
2020	BOS	MLB	27	4.29	21.21	112	0.0	97.4	50.0%	36.9%	
2021 FS	*BOS*	*MLB*	*28*	*1.54*	*4.94*	*111*	*-0.1*	*97.4*	*50.0%*	*36.9%*	*37.6%*

Robinson Leyer, continued

Pitch Shape vs LHH

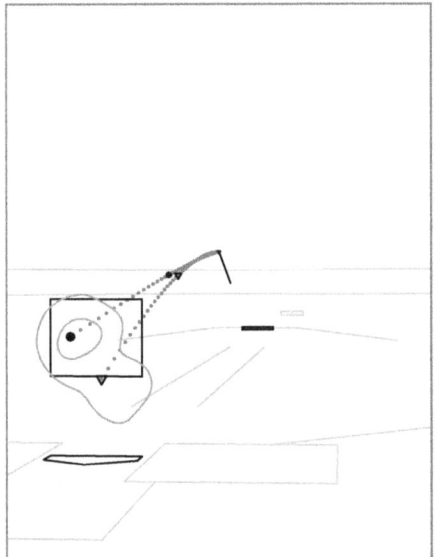

Pitch Shape vs RHH

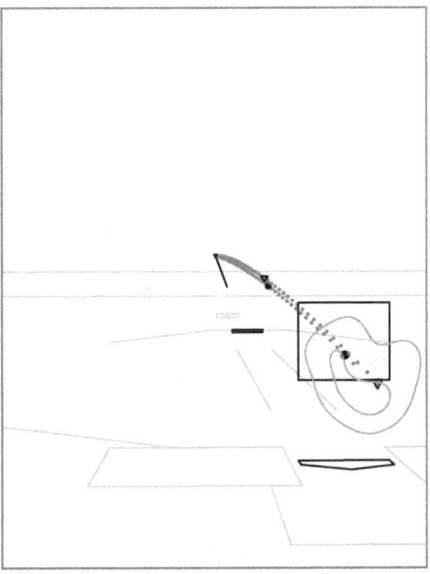

Type	Frequency	Velocity	H Movement	V Movement
● Fastball	50.0%	95.2 [108]	-5.2 [107]	-11.7 [110]
▽ Slider	50.0%	87.5 [116]	4.6 [98]	-28.1 [116]

Chris Mazza RHP

Born: 10/17/89   Age: 31   Bats: R   Throws: R
Height: 6'4"   Weight: 190   Origin: Round 27, 2011 Draft (#838 overall)

YEAR	TEAM	LVL	AGE	W	L	SV	G	GS	IP	H	HR	BB/9	K/9	K	GB%	BABIP
2018	ARK	AA	28	1	0	0	4	4	27	15	1	1.3	7.7	23	62.5%	.197
2018	JAX	AA	28	0	0	0	2	0	6^1	8	2	2.8	2.8	2	39.1%	.286
2018	NO	AAA	28	1	1	0	7	0	16	18	4	4.5	7.9	14	58.8%	.298
2019	BNG	AA	29	0	2	0	4	4	23^2	26	0	3.0	8.0	21	47.9%	.356
2019	SYR	AAA	29	3	3	0	14	13	76	65	6	2.1	7.3	62	56.9%	.282
2019	NYM	MLB	29	1	1	0	9	0	16^1	21	0	2.8	6.1	11	40.7%	.389
2020	BOS	MLB	30	1	2	0	9	6	30	34	3	4.5	8.7	29	34.4%	.356
2021 FS	*BOS*	*MLB*	*31*	*9*	*9*	*0*	*26*	*26*	*150*	*149*	*23*	*3.3*	*7.4*	*123*	*44.5%*	*.288*
2021 DC	*BOS*	*MLB*	*31*	*3*	*3*	*0*	*25*	*6*	*45.7*	*45*	*7*	*3.3*	*7.4*	*37*	*44.5%*	*.288*

Comparables: Murphy Smith, Chad Bettis, Casey Lawrence

    Mazza has made it to the majors two years in a row now, and he didn't take the easy way up. A 2011 draftee who had to climb his way back to relevance through stints in the independent Pacific and Atlantic Leagues, he's also been a Rule 5 draft pick (2018, Mets via Mariners) and been DFAd twice. Claimed by the Sox off waivers last winter, Mazza had the honor of giving up 2020's biggest moonshot, a prodigious 495-foot blast to Ronald Acuña Jr. that may not have landed as of printing. He also had the honor of pitching "well" enough to place as the seventh-best Red Sox pitcher by both WARP and DRA, which tells you all you need to know about Boston's historically bad staff.

YEAR	TEAM	LVL	AGE	WHIP	ERA	DRA-	WARP	MPH	FB%	WHF	CSP
2018	ARK	AA	28	0.70	1.33	78	0.4				
2018	JAX	AA	28	1.58	4.26	126	-0.1				
2018	NO	AAA	28	1.62	3.94	73	0.3				
2019	BNG	AA	29	1.44	3.42	119	-0.2				
2019	SYR	AAA	29	1.09	3.67	57	2.9				
2019	NYM	MLB	29	1.59	5.51	158	-0.4	93.3	78.4%	17.9%	
2020	BOS	MLB	30	1.63	4.80	99	0.3	93.8	68.9%	28.9%	
2021 FS	*BOS*	*MLB*	*31*	*1.37*	*4.68*	*105*	*1.0*	*93.7*	*71.4%*	*26.1%*	*47.2%*
2021 DC	*BOS*	*MLB*	*31*	*1.37*	*4.68*	*105*	*0.2*	*93.7*	*71.4%*	*26.1%*	*47.2%*

Chris Mazza, continued

Pitch Shape vs LHH

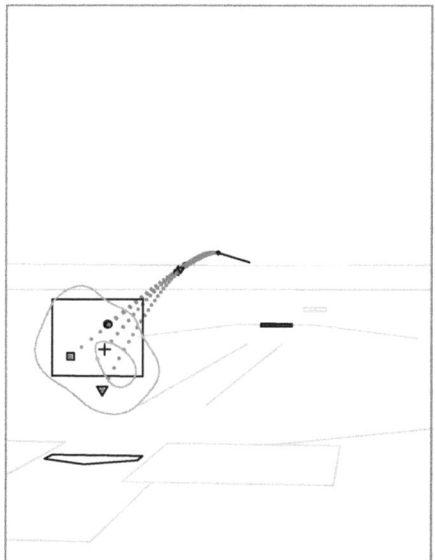

Pitch Shape vs RHH

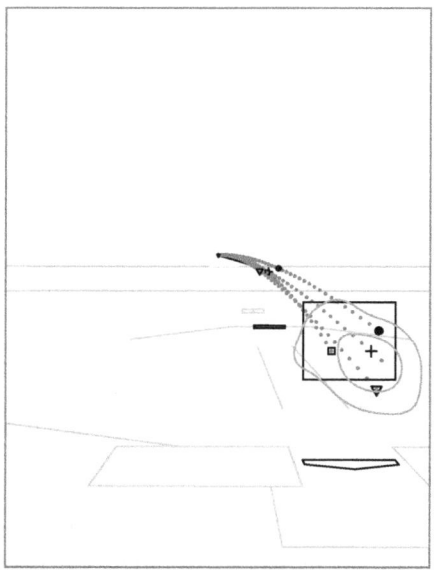

Type	Frequency	Velocity	H Movement	V Movement
● Fastball	16.7%	92.6 [100]	-7.3 [97]	-18.7 [90]
☐ Sinker	22.1%	91.9 [97]	-14.8 [87]	-24.9 [86]
+ Cutter	29.9%	88.7 [102]	2.5 [104]	-25.3 [96]
▲ Changeup	3.2%	84.9 [99]	-8.5 [117]	-34.1 [82]
▽ Slider	27.9%	82.4 [93]	6.9 [106]	-36.1 [93]

Adam Ottavino RHP

Born: 11/22/85 Age: 35 Bats: S Throws: R
Height: 6'5" Weight: 246 Origin: Round 1, 2006 Draft (#30 overall)

YEAR	TEAM	LVL	AGE	W	L	SV	G	GS	IP	H	HR	BB/9	K/9	K	GB%	BABIP
2018	COL	MLB	32	6	4	6	75	0	77^2	41	5	4.2	13.0	112	42.2%	.243
2019	NYY	MLB	33	6	5	2	73	0	66^1	47	5	5.4	11.9	88	40.1%	.286
2020	NYY	MLB	34	2	3	0	24	0	18^1	20	2	4.4	12.3	25	52.0%	.375
2021 FS	BOS	MLB	35	2	2	7	57	0	50	41	5	5.2	10.9	60	44.0%	.298
2021 DC	BOS	MLB	35	2	2	7	56	0	61	50	6	5.2	10.9	74	44.0%	.298

Comparables: David Hernandez, Wade Davis, Steve Cishek

Analyzing how any player performed in a 60-game sample is challenging work; trying to figure out what it means for a reliever is like trying to figure out the names of those angels dancing on the head of William Sclater's metaphorical pin. In Ottavino's case, it doesn't take an otherworldly magnifying glass and calipers to figure out why his 2020 numbers were terrible. On September 7, Ottavino was hung out to dry in a 12-7 loss against the Blue Jays in a Triple-A bandbox that was hosting games only because Canada had closed its borders to Major League Baseball. Take away that ghastly, zero-inning, six-earned-run outing and Ottavino had a 2.95 ERA. Even with that nightmarish contest on his resume, he posted a 3.35 DRA, or a better rate than he did in his Yankee debut in 2019. He was fine, in other words, and should continue to be a key asset for New York in the final season of his three-year, $27 million pact.

YEAR	TEAM	LVL	AGE	WHIP	ERA	DRA-	WARP	MPH	FB%	WHF	CSP
2018	COL	MLB	32	0.99	2.43	67	1.7	95.7	43.1%	32.9%	
2019	NYY	MLB	33	1.31	1.90	74	1.2	95.6	41.5%	29.9%	
2020	NYY	MLB	34	1.58	5.89	72	0.4	95.0	44.8%	26.5%	
2021 FS	BOS	MLB	35	1.42	3.92	92	0.5	95.5	42.7%	30.0%	49.3%
2021 DC	BOS	MLB	35	1.42	3.92	92	0.6	95.5	42.7%	30.0%	49.3%

Adam Ottavino, continued

Pitch Shape vs LHH

Pitch Shape vs RHH

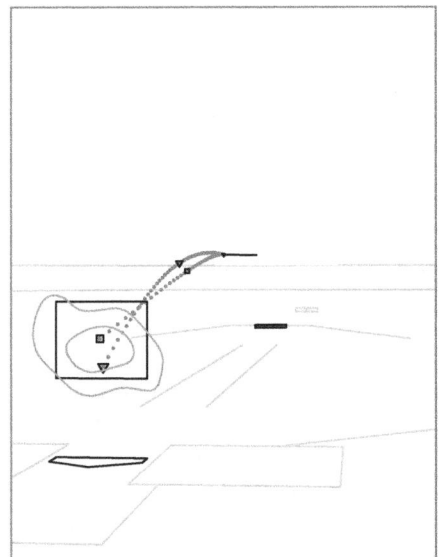
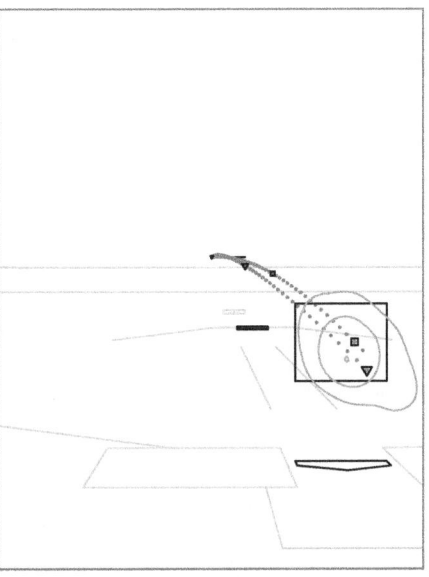

Type	Frequency	Velocity	H Movement	V Movement
☐ Sinker	44.5%	93.5 [106]	-13.2 [99]	-22.2 [95]
+ Cutter	5.0%	86.3 [87]	1.9 [100]	-24.1 [101]
▲ Changeup	3.8%	88.2 [112]	-11.2 [103]	-29.1 [96]
▽ Slider	46.3%	81 [87]	16.2 [141]	-36.4 [92]

Martín Pérez LHP

Born: 04/04/91 Age: 30 Bats: L Throws: L
Height: 6'0" Weight: 200 Origin: International Free Agent, 2007

YEAR	TEAM	LVL	AGE	W	L	SV	G	GS	IP	H	HR	BB/9	K/9	K	GB%	BABIP
2018	FRI	AA	27	1	0	0	1	1	6	2	0	4.5	6.0	4	58.8%	.118
2018	RR	AAA	27	1	0	0	1	1	6^1	6	1	0.0	8.5	6	72.2%	.294
2018	TEX	MLB	27	2	7	0	22	15	85^1	116	16	3.8	5.5	52	50.8%	.345
2019	MIN	MLB	28	10	7	0	32	29	165^1	184	23	3.6	7.3	135	47.9%	.318
2020	BOS	MLB	29	3	5	0	12	12	62	55	8	4.1	6.7	46	38.4%	.267
2021 FS	BOS	MLB	30	9	9	0	26	26	150	154	20	3.5	7.3	121	44.3%	.297
2021 DC	BOS	MLB	30	8	8	0	25	25	134.7	138	18	3.5	7.3	109	44.3%	.297

Comparables: Jordan Lyles, Kendall Graveman, Tyler Chatwood

Perez perfectly represents the good, bad and ugly of Boston's newfound approach to roster-building. First, the positives: taking low-cost, medium-upside fliers on players is a smart way to round out a team. In Perez, the Sox found a back-of-the-rotation workhorse who paced the team in innings while making just $6 million. Onto the bad: when you're overly reliant on Perez-type fliers, you rob your team of any real upside. It's embarrassing that Perez was Boston's second-best starter by most metrics, yet finished 75th in DRA among pitchers with at least 50 IP, behind stalwarts like Alec Mills and Kris Bubic. And here's the truly ugly part: despite Perez's modestly useful performance (by ERA) and very useful price tag, the Sox still declined his $6.25 million option for 2021, undoubtedly hoping to eke more value out of a cheaper arm. Perez may be little more than an innings-eater, but no matter how much you value "financial flexibility," you've gotta pay *someone* to actually eat said innings.

YEAR	TEAM	LVL	AGE	WHIP	ERA	DRA-	WARP	MPH	FB%	WHF	CSP
2018	FRI	AA	27	0.83	0.00	131	-0.1				
2018	RR	AAA	27	0.95	1.42	62	0.2				
2018	TEX	MLB	27	1.78	6.22	163	-2.0	95.2	67.3%	17.9%	
2019	MIN	MLB	28	1.52	5.12	129	-1.0	95.8	73.2%	21.7%	
2020	BOS	MLB	29	1.34	4.50	133	-0.6	94.1	65.1%	22.3%	
2021 FS	BOS	MLB	30	1.42	4.41	105	1.0	95.2	69.8%	21.4%	46.8%
2021 DC	BOS	MLB	30	1.42	4.41	105	0.9	95.2	69.8%	21.4%	46.8%

Martín Pérez, continued

Pitch Shape vs LHH

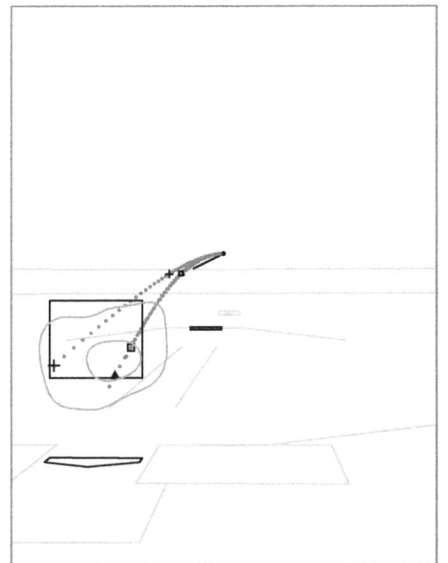

Pitch Shape vs RHH

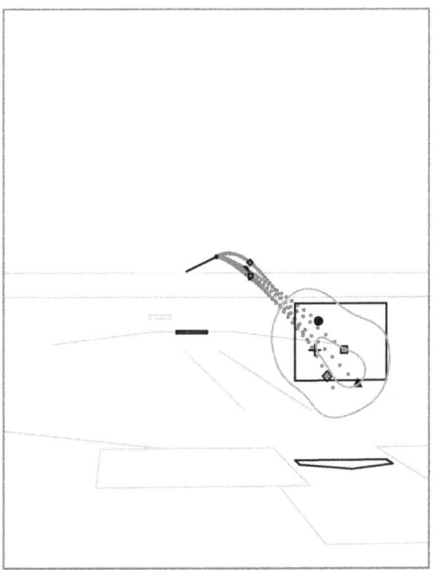

Type	Frequency	Velocity	H Movement	V Movement
● Fastball	14.5%	92.4 [99]	9.3 [87]	-15.5 [99]
□ Sinker	19.0%	92.1 [98]	15 [86]	-20.1 [101]
+ Cutter	31.6%	89 [104]	0.6 [84]	-21.6 [110]
▲ Changeup	25.6%	83.8 [95]	12.9 [94]	-26.8 [102]
◇ Curveball	9.4%	77.9 [97]	-4.8 [89]	-45.1 [107]

Nick Pivetta RHP

Born: 02/14/93 Age: 28 Bats: R Throws: R
Height: 6'5" Weight: 214 Origin: Round 4, 2013 Draft (#136 overall)

YEAR	TEAM	LVL	AGE	W	L	SV	G	GS	IP	H	HR	BB/9	K/9	K	GB%	BABIP
2018	PHI	MLB	25	7	14	0	33	32	164	163	24	2.8	10.3	188	46.9%	.333
2019	LHV	AAA	26	5	1	0	9	6	41	23	2	4.8	12.7	58	50.6%	.256
2019	PHI	MLB	26	4	6	1	30	13	93²	103	20	3.7	8.6	89	42.6%	.313
2020	BOS	MLB	27	2	0	0	5	2	15²	18	4	3.4	9.8	17	27.7%	.326
2021 FS	BOS	MLB	28	9	8	0	26	26	150	133	19	3.7	9.9	164	41.3%	.296
2021 DC	BOS	MLB	28	7	5	0	31	16	103.7	92	13	3.7	9.9	114	41.3%	.296

Comparables: Jon Gray, Jakob Junis, Vince Velasquez

In September 2018, the Red Sox were putting the finishing touches on a 108-win season. By September 2020, they were manipulating Pivetta's service time. Oh, how the mighty have fallen. To be fair to Chaim Bloom and co., Pivetta was a decent get for a few dozen innings of Brandon Workman and Heath Hembree. He's big, throws hard, has some track record of major-league success and is just young enough that you can still talk yourself into a pending breakout. But at this point Pivetta's performance speaks for itself, and he continues to prove that velocity alone isn't enough to beat big-league hitters. Perhaps a change of scenery and work with a new staff will unlock Pivetta's potential, but odds are this will go down as yet another example of the Red Sox being lured by the siren song of a pitcher with Great Stuff (TM) and no idea where it's going.

YEAR	TEAM	LVL	AGE	WHIP	ERA	DRA-	WARP	MPH	FB%	WHF	CSP
2018	PHI	MLB	25	1.30	4.77	75	3.6	96.7	58.9%	28.0%	
2019	LHV	AAA	26	1.10	3.07	40	1.9				
2019	PHI	MLB	26	1.52	5.38	103	0.6	96.8	51.1%	24.7%	
2020	BOS	MLB	27	1.53	6.89	121	0.0	94.6	49.3%	24.3%	
2021 FS	BOS	MLB	28	1.31	3.72	90	2.3	96.5	54.0%	26.0%	48.6%
2021 DC	BOS	MLB	28	1.31	3.72	90	1.5	96.5	54.0%	26.0%	48.6%

Nick Pivetta, continued

Pitch Shape vs LHH

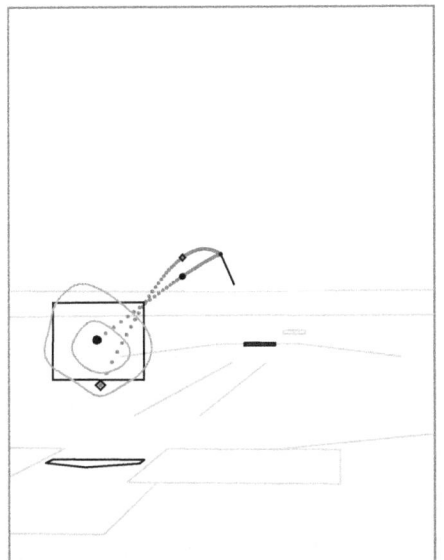

Pitch Shape vs RHH

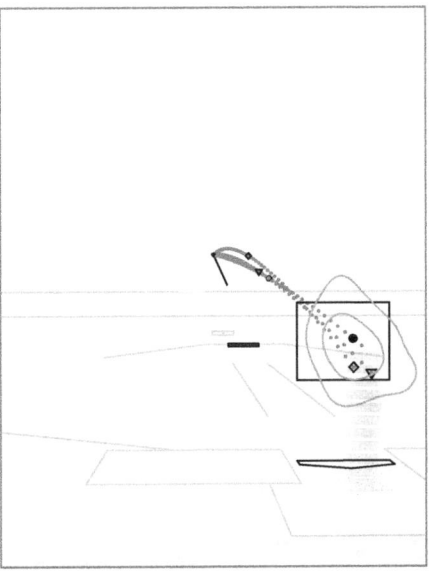

Type	Frequency	Velocity	H Movement	V Movement
● Fastball	49.3%	93 [101]	-7 [99]	-11.2 [111]
▲ Changeup	6.2%	86 [103]	-11.8 [100]	-24.5 [108]
▽ Slider	19.0%	85.6 [107]	5.4 [100]	-31.2 [107]
◇ Curveball	24.5%	79.9 [105]	8 [102]	-50.5 [95]

Garrett Richards   RHP

Born: 05/27/88   Age: 33   Bats: R   Throws: R
Height: 6'2"   Weight: 210   Origin: Round 1, 2009 Draft (#42 overall)

YEAR	TEAM	LVL	AGE	W	L	SV	G	GS	IP	H	HR	BB/9	K/9	K	GB%	BABIP
2018	LAA	MLB	30	5	4	0	16	16	76^1	64	11	4.0	10.3	87	50.0%	.279
2019	LE	HI-A	31	0	1	0	3	3	6^2	8	1	10.8	10.8	8	47.4%	.389
2019	SD	MLB	31	0	1	0	3	3	8^2	10	2	6.2	11.4	11	41.7%	.381
2020	SD	MLB	32	2	2	0	14	10	51^1	47	7	3.0	8.1	46	40.5%	.284
2021 FS	BOS	MLB	33	9	8	0	26	26	150	141	19	4.0	8.9	147	44.5%	.297
2021 DC	BOS	MLB	33	6	6	0	21	21	101	95	12	4.0	8.9	99	44.5%	.297

Comparables: Tyson Ross, Luis Tiant, Chris Short

Richards' name doesn't come up as frequently in those "what-if he had stayed healthy" conversations as, say, Troy Tulowitzki's or Grady Sizemore's, but it's still a shame that injuries had limited him to just 31 starts over four seasons following his high-quality performances in 2014-15. For that reason it was heartening to see him stay more or less healthy in 2020, and to do so while being reasonably productive. Richards' home-run rate remained on the high side, and it's worth wondering if we were getting a glimpse of his future when the Padres shifted him to the bullpen late in the year. Pitching relief beats wondering about the career you might have had.

YEAR	TEAM	LVL	AGE	WHIP	ERA	DRA-	WARP	MPH	FB%	WHF	CSP
2018	LAA	MLB	30	1.28	3.66	83	1.4	97.5	50.4%	28.5%	
2019	LE	HI-A	31	2.40	8.10	184	-0.3				
2019	SD	MLB	31	1.85	8.31	77	0.2	96.2	58.0%	30.5%	
2020	SD	MLB	32	1.25	4.03	99	0.5	96.5	54.8%	25.9%	
2021 FS	BOS	MLB	33	1.38	4.07	98	1.6	96.8	53.6%	27.1%	47.0%
2021 DC	BOS	MLB	33	1.38	4.07	98	1.1	96.8	53.6%	27.1%	47.0%

Garrett Richards, continued

Pitch Shape vs LHH

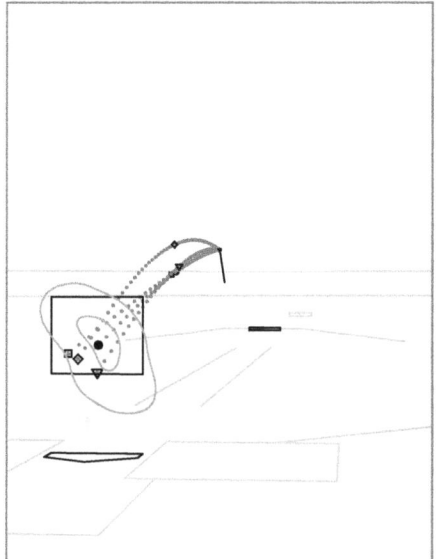

Pitch Shape vs RHH

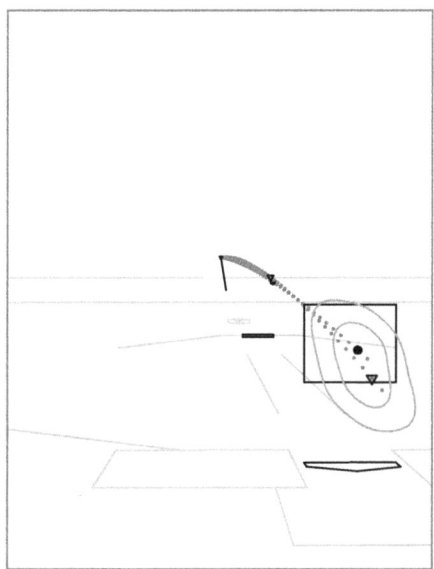

Type	Frequency	Velocity	H Movement	V Movement
● Fastball	44.4%	95.2 [108]	0.6 [135]	-17.4 [94]
□ Sinker	10.3%	95.3 [115]	-7.9 [138]	-18 [108]
▽ Slider	37.7%	88.5 [120]	2.8 [91]	-33.7 [100]
◇ Curveball	7.5%	80 [106]	9.7 [109]	-57.1 [81]

Boston Red Sox 2021

Jeffrey Springs LHP
Born: 09/20/92 Age: 28 Bats: L Throws: L
Height: 6'3" Weight: 218 Origin: Round 30, 2015 Draft (#888 overall)

YEAR	TEAM	LVL	AGE	W	L	SV	G	GS	IP	H	HR	BB/9	K/9	K	GB%	BABIP
2018	FRI	AA	25	3	2	1	20	0	37^1	39	2	1.7	16.4	68	39.7%	.487
2018	RR	AAA	25	1	2	1	13	0	19^1	12	0	5.6	14.0	30	44.4%	.333
2018	TEX	MLB	25	1	1	0	18	2	32	32	4	3.9	8.7	31	31.6%	.311
2019	NAS	AAA	26	3	0	0	6	0	7	6	1	0.0	15.4	12	42.9%	.417
2019	TEX	MLB	26	4	1	0	25	0	32^1	38	4	6.4	8.9	32	25.3%	.358
2020	BOS	MLB	27	0	2	0	16	0	20^1	30	5	3.1	12.4	28	36.5%	.431
2021 FS	*BOS*	*MLB*	*28*	*2*	*2*	*0*	*57*	*0*	*50*	*44*	*7*	*4.0*	*10.8*	*59*	*34.5%*	*.298*
2021 DC	*BOS*	*MLB*	*28*	*2*	*2*	*0*	*42*	*0*	*26.3*	*23*	*4*	*4.0*	*10.8*	*31*	*34.5%*	*.298*

Comparables: Austin Davis, Stephen Tarpley, Dillon Peters

Acquired for Sam Travis back in January 2020, Springs is a tall, lanky left-hander who hasn't pitched well enough to earn spots in the Rangers' or Red Sox's bullpens over the past few years. There's no need to pile on.

YEAR	TEAM	LVL	AGE	WHIP	ERA	DRA-	WARP	MPH	FB%	WHF	CSP
2018	FRI	AA	25	1.23	4.82	40	1.3				
2018	RR	AAA	25	1.24	2.79	42	0.7				
2018	TEX	MLB	25	1.44	3.38	132	-0.4	93.1	62.7%	27.1%	
2019	NAS	AAA	26	0.86	3.86	32	0.3				
2019	TEX	MLB	26	1.89	6.40	163	-0.9	93.6	58.0%	30.2%	
2020	BOS	MLB	27	1.82	7.08	81	0.4	93.4	46.9%	37.6%	
2021 FS	*BOS*	*MLB*	*28*	*1.33*	*4.22*	*95*	*0.4*	*93.4*	*54.5%*	*32.5%*	*50.0%*
2021 DC	*BOS*	*MLB*	*28*	*1.33*	*4.22*	*95*	*0.2*	*93.4*	*54.5%*	*32.5%*	*50.0%*

Jeffrey Springs, continued

Pitch Shape vs LHH

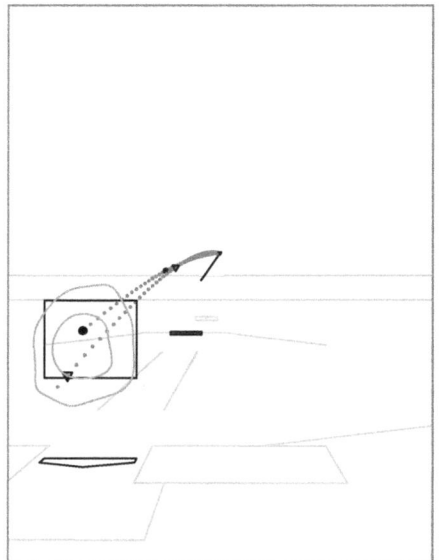

Pitch Shape vs RHH

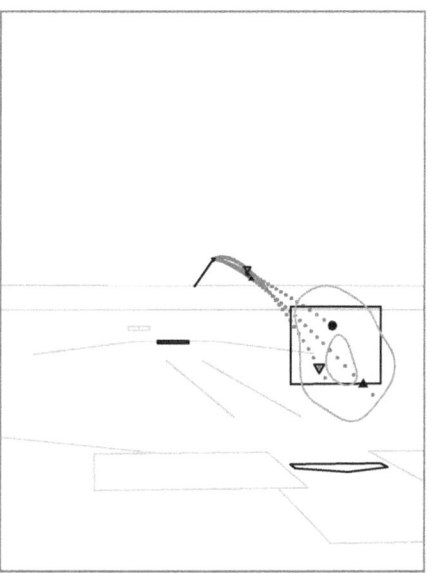

Type	Frequency	Velocity	H Movement	V Movement
● Fastball	46.5%	92.3 [99]	9.1 [88]	-14 [103]
▲ Changeup	25.7%	81.7 [86]	9.5 [111]	-28 [99]
▽ Slider	26.9%	83.1 [96]	-3.7 [94]	-36.6 [92]

Phillips Valdez   RHP

Born: 11/16/91   Age: 29   Bats: R   Throws: R
Height: 6'2"   Weight: 160   Origin: International Free Agent, 2008

YEAR	TEAM	LVL	AGE	W	L	SV	G	GS	IP	H	HR	BB/9	K/9	K	GB%	BABIP
2018	HBG	AA	26	0	0	0	5	0	10^2	9	0	1.7	6.8	8	43.3%	.300
2018	SYR	AAA	26	6	7	0	26	19	124^1	111	10	3.2	6.9	96	58.0%	.281
2019	NAS	AAA	27	1	7	1	26	14	78^2	87	10	4.1	7.4	65	53.3%	.314
2019	TEX	MLB	27	0	0	0	11	0	16	17	3	5.1	10.1	18	52.2%	.326
2020	BOS	MLB	28	1	1	0	24	0	30^1	33	3	4.7	8.9	30	46.6%	.353
2021 FS	BOS	MLB	29	2	3	0	57	0	50	50	5	4.6	8.2	45	49.7%	.309
2021 DC	BOS	MLB	29	2	2	0	48	0	48.7	49	5	4.6	8.2	44	49.7%	.309

Comparables: Mike Mayers, Glenn Sparkman, Kevin McCarthy

Valdez should be nicknamed "Exxon" because he paid no real price (3.26 ERA) for courting disaster (33 hits allowed in 30 1/3 innings).

YEAR	TEAM	LVL	AGE	WHIP	ERA	DRA-	WARP	MPH	FB%	WHF	CSP
2018	HBG	AA	26	1.03	2.53	55	0.3				
2018	SYR	AAA	26	1.25	2.75	83	2.0				
2019	NAS	AAA	27	1.56	4.92	96	1.4				
2019	TEX	MLB	27	1.62	3.94	93	0.1	94.1	58.4%	21.8%	
2020	BOS	MLB	28	1.62	3.26	94	0.4	94.0	45.2%	27.7%	
2021 FS	BOS	MLB	29	1.51	4.78	108	0.0	94.0	48.8%	26.1%	46.5%
2021 DC	BOS	MLB	29	1.51	4.78	108	0.0	94.0	48.8%	26.1%	46.5%

Phillips Valdez, continued

Pitch Shape vs LHH

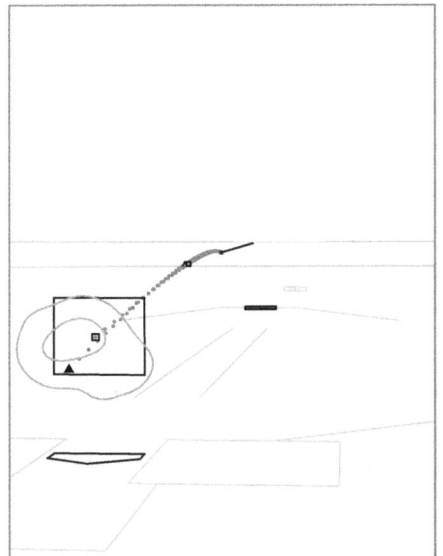

Pitch Shape vs RHH

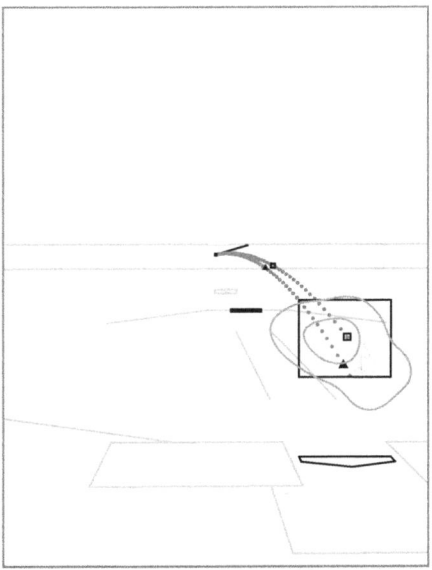

Type	Frequency	Velocity	H Movement	V Movement
☐ Sinker	45.2%	92.4 [100]	-17.2 [70]	-26.8 [80]
▲ Changeup	48.9%	85.2 [100]	-14.2 [87]	-34.7 [80]
▽ Slider	5.9%	81.7 [90]	5 [99]	-38.3 [87]

Marcus Walden RHP

Born: 09/13/88   Age: 32   Bats: R   Throws: R
Height: 5'10"   Weight: 198   Origin: Round 9, 2007 Draft (#295 overall)

YEAR	TEAM	LVL	AGE	W	L	SV	G	GS	IP	H	HR	BB/9	K/9	K	GB%	BABIP
2018	WOR	AAA	29	0	4	2	18	5	32²	44	2	4.7	6.6	24	50.4%	.368
2018	BOS	MLB	29	0	0	1	8	0	14²	14	0	1.8	8.6	14	58.5%	.341
2019	BOS	MLB	30	9	2	2	70	0	78	61	6	3.7	8.8	76	55.1%	.266
2020	BOS	MLB	31	0	2	1	15	0	13¹	23	5	6.1	6.8	10	40.4%	.383
2021 FS	BOS	MLB	32	2	2	0	57	0	50	48	6	4.1	7.7	42	49.2%	.292
2021 DC	BOS	MLB	32	2	2	0	48	0	18	17	2	4.1	7.7	15	49.2%	.292

Comparables: Tommy Layne, Jeff Manship, Justin Grimm

There was stiff competition for the honorific of "most disappointing Red Sox pitcher" last season, but Walden deserves serious consideration. After quietly serving as one of Boston's best relievers in 2019, Walden loudly fell apart. His strikeout rate fell while his walk and homer rates jumped. He threw his four-seam fastball and his slider less in favor of a two-seamer, and the results were disastrous—per Baseball Savant, opponents hit .355 off his cutter and .455 off his sinker. 2020 was a year full of disappointing but small samples, and it'd be short-sighted to write Walden off after just 13 1/3 bad innings. At the same time it's not as if he has a long track record of success, and careers for relievers like Walden can be rather ephemeral.

YEAR	TEAM	LVL	AGE	WHIP	ERA	DRA-	WARP	MPH	FB%	WHF	CSP
2018	WOR	AAA	29	1.87	4.96	94	0.2				
2018	BOS	MLB	29	1.16	3.68	70	0.3	95.7	45.1%	27.3%	
2019	BOS	MLB	30	1.19	3.81	78	1.3	95.7	34.8%	28.9%	
2020	BOS	MLB	31	2.40	9.45	157	-0.3	93.8	36.5%	18.4%	
2021 FS	BOS	MLB	32	1.43	4.37	103	0.2	95.3	35.8%	26.3%	43.7%
2021 DC	BOS	MLB	32	1.43	4.37	103	0.1	95.3	35.8%	26.3%	43.7%

Marcus Walden, continued

Pitch Shape vs LHH

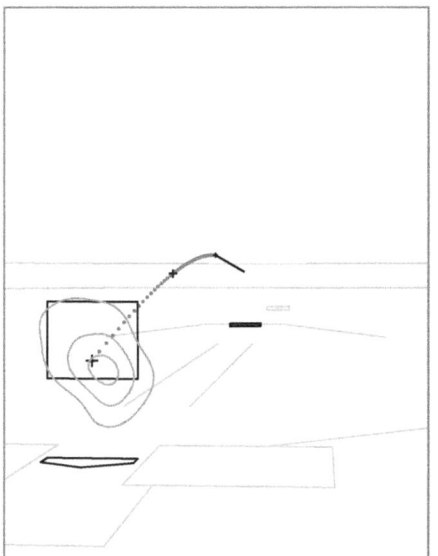

Pitch Shape vs RHH

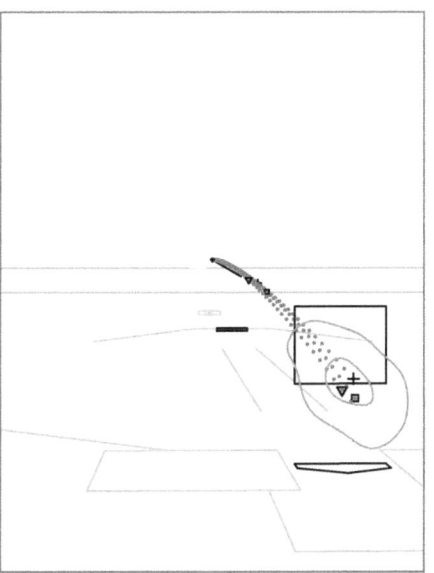

Type	Frequency	Velocity	H Movement	V Movement
● Fastball	11.2%	92.8 [101]	-1.5 [125]	-19.5 [88]
□ Sinker	25.3%	92.9 [102]	-7.7 [139]	-23 [92]
+ Cutter	42.5%	90.1 [111]	2.2 [102]	-24.7 [98]
▽ Slider	21.1%	84.8 [104]	7.2 [107]	-34.3 [98]

Ryan Weber RHP

Born: 08/12/90   Age: 30   Bats: R   Throws: R
Height: 6'1"   Weight: 175   Origin: Round 22, 2009 Draft (#658 overall)

YEAR	TEAM	LVL	AGE	W	L	SV	G	GS	IP	H	HR	BB/9	K/9	K	GB%	BABIP
2018	DUR	AAA	27	9	6	1	25	18	115^1	117	9	1.8	6.5	83	53.8%	.305
2018	TB	MLB	27	0	1	0	2	0	5^1	5	0	3.4	1.7	1	52.4%	.238
2019	WOR	AAA	28	1	5	0	16	16	78	86	9	2.9	7.3	63	53.3%	.328
2019	BOS	MLB	28	2	4	0	18	3	40^2	48	5	1.8	6.4	29	48.9%	.319
2020	BOS	MLB	29	1	3	0	17	5	43	44	8	2.9	5.7	27	53.2%	.273
2021 FS	BOS	MLB	30	2	2	0	57	0	50	52	6	2.3	6.3	35	51.5%	.295

Comparables: Casey Sadler, Tyler Duffey, Chris Stratton

Weber is a spare tire; useful enough in a pinch, but only designed to get you to the next exit. Since 2015, he's proven to possess the command and craftiness needed to survive for a few dozen innings at a time, but lack the talent required to offer much else. We have over 100 innings telling us Weber is the platonic ideal of a Quad-A pitcher, yet the Sox started the season banking on him to fill a spot in the rotation. You could argue that he disappointed, but that's not really fair—he did what he's always done, and what he's always done just isn't enough. If your plan is to use Weber for spot starts and long relief outings, you've adequately prepared to face some bumps in the road. If you start a long road trip with Weber on one of your rims, well, maybe you shouldn't be the one driving.

YEAR	TEAM	LVL	AGE	WHIP	ERA	DRA-	WARP	MPH	FB%	WHF	CSP
2018	DUR	AAA	27	1.21	2.73	95	1.0				
2018	TB	MLB	27	1.31	5.06	156	-0.1	90.0	74.3%	9.1%	
2019	WOR	AAA	28	1.42	4.50	100	1.4				
2019	BOS	MLB	28	1.38	5.09	102	0.2	90.8	52.7%	14.6%	
2020	BOS	MLB	29	1.35	4.40	110	0.1	90.2	50.9%	15.0%	
2021 FS	BOS	MLB	30	1.30	4.05	99	0.3	90.4	52.1%	14.7%	49.9%

Ryan Weber, continued

Pitch Shape vs LHH

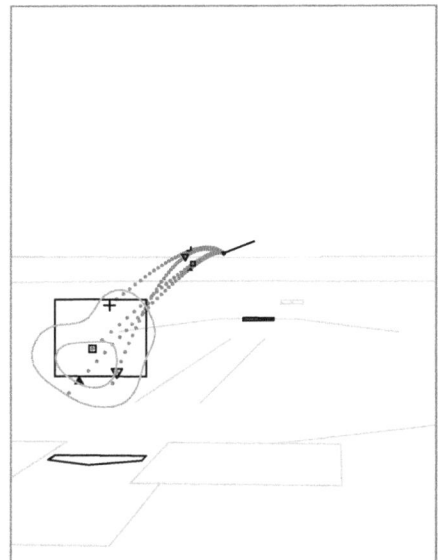

Pitch Shape vs RHH

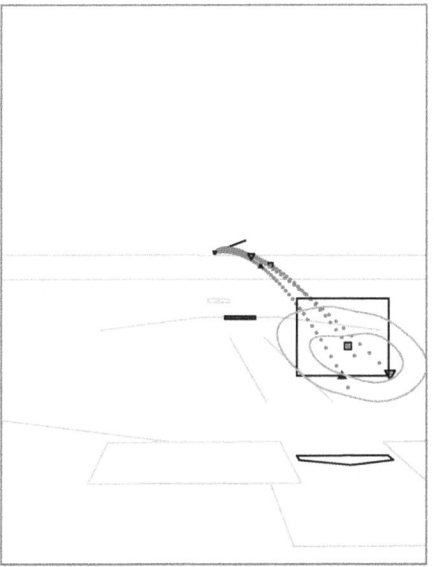

Type	Frequency	Velocity	H Movement	V Movement
☐ Sinker	50.9%	88.8 [81]	-16.8 [73]	-30.5 [68]
+ Cutter	9.6%	86.3 [87]	-3.8 [63]	-28.4 [84]
▲ Changeup	17.8%	81.8 [87]	-13.9 [89]	-35.2 [79]
▽ Slider	16.6%	77.7 [72]	15.8 [140]	-46.2 [64]
◇ Curveball	5.1%	74.5 [84]	14.4 [128]	-56.1 [83]

Boston Red Sox 2021

PLAYER COMMENTS WITHOUT GRAPHS

Triston Casas   3B
Born: 01/15/00   Age: 21   Bats: L   Throws: R
Height: 6'4"   Weight: 238   Origin: Round 1, 2018 Draft (#26 overall)

YEAR	TEAM	LVL	AGE	PA	R	2B	3B	HR	RBI	BB	K	SB	CS	AVG/OBP/SLG
2018	RSX	ROK	18	5	0	0	0	0	0	1	2	0	0	.000/.200/.000
2019	GVL	LO-A	19	493	64	25	5	19	78	58	116	3	2	.254/.349/.472
2019	SAL	HI-A	19	7	2	1	0	1	3	0	2	0	0	.429/.429/1.000
2021 FS	BOS	MLB	21	600	52	23	3	14	59	37	197	0	0	.200/.257/.333

Comparables: Lars Anderson, Mike Carp, Anthony Rizzo

Good news was hard to come by for the Red Sox last season, but most updates about Casas served as exceptions to that rule. Boston's 2018 first-round pick impressed with his size and power as he continued to grow into a massive 6-foot-5, 250-pound frame. What's even more encouraging is how Casas appeared to gain selectivity at the plate while facing relatively advanced pitching at Boston's alternate camp, perhaps in tribute to his self-proclaimed hero, Joey Votto. Drafting a first base prospect is always a risky proposition, but Casas is emerging as a potential prototypical first-division cold corner power bat. He should start the year as a 21-year-old in Double-A, meaning Green Monsters in the mirror may be closer than they appear.

YEAR	TEAM	LVL	AGE	PA	DRC+	BABIP	BRR	FRAA	WARP
2018	RSX	ROK	18	5		.000			
2019	GVL	LO-A	19	493	144	.300	-0.9	1B(94): -4.7, 3B(8): -1.2	2.1
2019	SAL	HI-A	19	7	158	.500	0.1	1B(2): -0.0	0.1
2021 FS	BOS	MLB	21	600	60	.280	-0.6	1B -2, 3B -1	-2.6

Rusney Castillo CF

Born: 07/09/87 Age: 34 Bats: R Throws: R
Height: 5'9" Weight: 207 Origin: International Free Agent, 2014

YEAR	TEAM	LVL	AGE	PA	R	2B	3B	HR	RBI	BB	K	SB	CS	AVG/OBP/SLG
2018	WOR	AAA	30	511	56	31	0	5	59	29	80	13	7	.319/.360/.416
2019	WOR	AAA	31	493	63	25	1	17	64	25	63	5	9	.278/.321/.448
2021 FS	BOS	MLB	33	600	55	26	1	14	61	30	136	1	1	.240/.287/.368

Comparables: Darnell McDonald, Chad Allen, Cory Sullivan

Odds are you and Castillo have more in common than you might think. For starters, you've probably made the same number of major league appearances over the past four seasons. Like Castillo, perhaps you settled down in a strange town you never envisioned yourself living in. And if someone offered you $72.5 million to kill your career and spend a half-decade in Pawtucket, well, just like Castillo, you'd probably grin and bear it. Castillo is finally free of the seven-year pact that long shackled him to Triple-A, but as a 33-year-old outfielder without a defining skill, he might remain mired there for non-contractual reasons. See, there's something else you and Castillo have in common: time doesn't wait for you.

YEAR	TEAM	LVL	AGE	PA	DRC+	BABIP	BRR	FRAA	WARP
2018	WOR	AAA	30	511	132	.372	1.2	CF(97): -4.6, RF(8): -0.4	2.3
2019	WOR	AAA	31	493	101	.291	-1.3	RF(82): 1.9, CF(25): 1.2	1.3
2021 FS	BOS	MLB	33	600	78	.293	-0.8	CF 1, RF 3	0.2

Franchy Cordero CF

Born: 09/02/94 Age: 26 Bats: L Throws: R
Height: 6'3" Weight: 226 Origin: International Free Agent, 2011

YEAR	TEAM	LVL	AGE	PA	R	2B	3B	HR	RBI	BB	K	SB	CS	AVG/OBP/SLG
2018	ELP	AAA	23	31	3	1	0	1	1	4	10	3	0	.259/.355/.407
2018	SD	MLB	23	154	19	5	1	7	19	14	55	5	2	.237/.307/.439
2019	ELP	AAA	24	51	7	2	1	3	8	4	19	0	0	.217/.294/.500
2019	SD	MLB	24	20	2	1	0	0	1	4	7	1	0	.333/.450/.400
2020	KC	MLB	25	42	7	3	0	2	7	4	4	1	0	.211/.286/.447
2021 FS	BOS	MLB	26	600	63	28	9	16	64	44	191	10	4	.237/.302/.411
2021 DC	BOS	MLB	26	449	47	21	7	12	48	33	143	7	3	.237/.302/.411

Comparables: Ruben Rivera, Alex Escobar, Ryan Thompson

When we meet Officer Nordberg in the opening minutes of The Naked Gun, he's shot several times, bangs his head on a pipe, burns his hand on a stove, falls against some wet paint, crushes his fingers under a window, stumbles headfirst into a wedding cake and steps into a bear trap before mercifully falling overboard. Cordero's injuries are nowhere near as comical, but they're almost as plentiful as poor, pitiful Nordberg's. Last year saw the third consecutive season he landed on the 60-day IL; this time around it was a sprained right wrist that put him on the shelf, but at least he made it back on the field. Small victories. As the Royals assemble their 2021 outfield, he will get every chance to contribute. All he has to do is … you know … stay healthy.

YEAR	TEAM	LVL	AGE	PA	DRC+	BABIP	BRR	FRAA	WARP
2018	ELP	AAA	23	31	66	.375	0.6	LF(3): -0.4, CF(3): -0.8	-0.1
2018	SD	MLB	23	154	72	.338	0.6	LF(22): 0.4, CF(11): -1.3, RF(4): -0.8	-0.2
2019	ELP	AAA	24	51	60	.292	0.5	CF(9): 0.6	0.0
2019	SD	MLB	24	20	74	.556	0.6	CF(5): -0.4, RF(4): -0.3	0.0
2020	KC	MLB	25	42	96	.188	0.3	RF(8): -0.5, CF(5): -0.5, LF(1): 0.2	0.0
2021 FS	BOS	MLB	26	600	89	.337	1.5	LF 7, CF 0	1.7
2021 DC	BOS	MLB	26	449	89	.337	1.1	LF 5, CF 0	1.2

Jeter Downs SS
Born: 07/27/98   Age: 22   Bats: R   Throws: R
Height: 5'11"   Weight: 195   Origin: Round 1, 2017 Draft (#32 overall)

YEAR	TEAM	LVL	AGE	PA	R	2B	3B	HR	RBI	BB	K	SB	CS	AVG/OBP/SLG
2018	DAY	LO-A	19	524	63	23	2	13	47	52	103	37	10	.257/.351/.402
2019	RC	HI-A	20	475	76	32	4	19	75	53	96	22	8	.269/.353/.506
2019	TUL	AA	20	56	14	2	0	5	11	6	10	1	0	.333/.429/.688
2021 FS	BOS	MLB	22	600	61	24	2	18	68	47	162	14	7	.226/.296/.385

Comparables: Addison Russell, Daniel Robertson, Lonnie Chisenhall

It's one thing to trade a franchise icon in order to save your billionaire owner a few bucks. It's another to ensure that the return for said icon includes a player named after the most hated rival in your team's history. It will be strange to see a Jeter manning an infield spot for the Red Sox, but we're headed that way in a hurry—Downs continued to impress at Boston's alternate camp, which means a big-league debut is likely right around the corner. He's not the toolsiest prospect in the world, but also lacks much in the way of a weakness. Downs is not a power hitter, but he's got enough pop to keep pitchers honest. He's not a true speedster, but he'll swipe a few bags. He's athletic enough to play a good second base, but should only slide over to short in a pinch. Essentially, Downs is the type of Role 55-ish everyday player Chaim Bloom collected in droves as part of Tampa's front office. He'll provide the Sox with an affordable, acceptable option for several years, though his moniker, involvement in the Mookie Betts trade, and status as the likely heir to Dustin Pedroia mean he'll face plenty of pressure.

YEAR	TEAM	LVL	AGE	PA	DRC+	BABIP	BRR	FRAA	WARP
2018	DAY	LO-A	19	524	121	.306	-1.6	2B(73): -2.9, SS(43): -9.3	0.8
2019	RC	HI-A	20	475	126	.302	4.1	SS(91): -4.0, 2B(10): -1.1	2.9
2019	TUL	AA	20	56	166	.333	0.8	SS(11): -0.4, 2B(1): -0.0	0.6
2021 FS	BOS	MLB	22	600	86	.286	1.1	SS -4, 2B -1	0.3

Jarren Duran OF
Born: 09/05/96   Age: 24   Bats: L   Throws: R
Height: 6'2"   Weight: 187   Origin: Round 7, 2018 Draft (#220 overall)

YEAR	TEAM	LVL	AGE	PA	R	2B	3B	HR	RBI	BB	K	SB	CS	AVG/OBP/SLG
2018	LOW	SS	21	168	28	5	10	2	20	11	26	12	4	.348/.393/.548
2018	GVL	LO-A	21	134	24	9	1	1	15	5	22	12	6	.367/.396/.477
2019	SAL	HI-A	22	226	49	13	3	4	19	23	44	18	5	.387/.456/.543
2019	POR	AA	22	352	41	11	5	1	19	23	84	28	8	.250/.309/.325
2021 FS	BOS	MLB	24	600	63	26	7	8	57	33	163	26	9	.248/.298/.368
2021 DC	BOS	MLB	24	33	3	1	0	0	3	1	8	0	1	.248/.298/.368

Comparables: Engel Beltre, Gorkys Hernández, Noel Cuevas

Boston Red Sox 2021

In a dark and miserable year, a lonely, desperate Red Sox Nation had but one thing to look forward to: #DuranSZN updates on Twitter. Sure, Duran may not be the Red Sox's *best* prospect, but he is arguably their most popular one. He's got a good story as a seventh-rounder now on the periphery of national prospect consciousness. He's got a fun skill set as a speedy outfielder who has reportedly added power to his game. And he's got the distinction of being one of the only prospects with any upside in the org's upper minors. We still don't know if Duran is an everyday player or more of a fourth outfielder, and 2020 deprived us of the chance to watch him face advanced pitching. But nearly every report on Duran from the Sox's alternate site was effusive in its praise. Barring a major influx of outfield talent, Boston figures to have need of his services at some point this year, which means your timeline could be flooded with #DuranSZN updates soon.

YEAR	TEAM	LVL	AGE	PA	DRC+	BABIP	BRR	FRAA	WARP
2018	LOW	SS	21	168	168	.406	0.4	2B(20): 4.9, CF(15): 0.1	1.6
2018	GVL	LO-A	21	134	163	.438	1.6	RF(30): -0.0	1.1
2019	SAL	HI-A	22	226	200	.480	3.4	CF(50): 0.2	3.3
2019	POR	AA	22	352	75	.335	5.1	CF(80): -3.3	0.5
2021 FS	BOS	MLB	24	600	78	.338	2.9	CF 2, 2B 0	0.6
2021 DC	BOS	MLB	24	33	78	.338	0.2	CF 0	0.0

Gilberto Jimenez   CF
Born: 07/08/00   Age: 20   Bats: S   Throws: R
Height: 5'11"   Weight: 160   Origin: International Free Agent, 2017

YEAR	TEAM	LVL	AGE	PA	R	2B	3B	HR	RBI	BB	K	SB	CS	AVG/OBP/SLG
2018	DSL RSB	ROK	17	284	42	10	8	0	22	19	40	16	14	.319/.384/.420
2019	LOW	SS	18	254	35	11	3	3	19	13	38	14	6	.359/.393/.470
2021 FS	BOS	MLB	20	600	48	23	4	7	51	29	160	17	10	.235/.278/.330

Comparables: Harold Ramirez, Franklin Barreto, Manuel Margot

For developmental prospects like Jimenez, the lack of a minor league season presented many challenges. Through no fault of his own, Jimenez was unable to hone his approach at the plate and budding switch-hitting abilities against live competition: a disappointment after winning the batting title at short-season Lowell in 2019. We don't know if he's added power or learned to walk more, and we don't know if he's improved his routes in center field. What we do know is that Jimenez took care of the stuff he could control, such as strength training and conditioning, as he reportedly showed up to instructionals looking bigger and stronger. If that translates to more pop for Jimenez he could become a top-100 prospect in short order, but until he gets to face live pitching, we're all in wait-and-see mode.

YEAR	TEAM	LVL	AGE	PA	DRC+	BABIP	BRR	FRAA	WARP
2018	DSL RSB	ROK	17	284		.378			
2019	LOW	SS	18	254	190	.413	1.2	CF(57): -9.8, LF(1): -0.1, RF(1): -0.1	1.9
2021 FS	BOS	MLB	20	600	67	.316	1.9	CF 2, RF 0	-0.3

Blaze Jordan 3B
Born: 12/19/02   Age: 18   Bats: R   Throws: R
Height: 6'2"   Weight: 220   Origin: Round 3, 2020 Draft (#89 overall)

    Popped with the 89th pick in the 2020 draft but signed to a massive overslot deal, Jordan has some of the best raw power in the minors and a halfway decent idea how to use it. That his name sounds like a Cody Bellinger-inspired series of Air Force Ones is but an added bonus.

Matthew Lugo SS
Born: 05/09/01   Age: 20   Bats: R   Throws: R
Height: 6'1"   Weight: 185   Origin: Round 2, 2019 Draft (#69 overall)

YEAR	TEAM	LVL	AGE	PA	R	2B	3B	HR	RBI	BB	K	SB	CS	AVG/OBP/SLG
2019	RSX	ROK	18	157	19	5	1	1	12	15	36	3	0	.257/.342/.331
2019	LOW	SS	18	8	0	0	0	0	1	0	2	0	0	.250/.250/.250
2021 FS	BOS	MLB	20	600	43	20	2	8	48	32	213	2	2	.188/.239/.279

Comparables: Tzu-Wei Lin, Gavin Lux, Luis Sardiñas

    Thanks to the lack of a minor league season, we don't know if toolsy shortstop prospect Lugo has started to make good on his potential. Sox fans are used to waiting on production from a Lugo at the six, at least.

YEAR	TEAM	LVL	AGE	PA	DRC+	BABIP	BRR	FRAA	WARP
2019	RSX	ROK	18	157		.340			
2019	LOW	SS	18	8	79	.333	-0.1	SS(2): -0.6	-0.1
2021 FS	BOS	MLB	20	600	41	.286	-0.3	SS -1	-2.9

Boston Red Sox 2021

Dustin Pedroia   2B
Born: 08/17/83   Age: 37   Bats: R   Throws: R
Height: 5'9"   Weight: 170   Origin: Round 2, 2004 Draft (#65 overall)

YEAR	TEAM	LVL	AGE	PA	R	2B	3B	HR	RBI	BB	K	SB	CS	AVG/OBP/SLG
2018	BOS	MLB	34	13	1	0	0	0	0	2	1	0	0	.091/.231/.091
2019	BOS	MLB	35	21	1	0	0	0	1	1	2	0	0	.100/.143/.100
2021 FS	BOS	MLB	37	600	59	26	0	10	58	55	97	6	3	.259/.332/.371

Comparables: Jose Vidro, Ian Kinsler, Davey Johnson

One way or another, 2021 will mark the end of Pedroia's career. The 8-year, $110-million extension he signed in June of 2013 once seemed team-friendly, a nod to Pedroia's twin desires to retire in Boston and to help his team at any cost. In reality, it's badly hamstrung the Sox in their self-imposed financial crunch: Pedey's made $44 million to play in just nine games over the past three seasons, and he's about to make $12 million more. We should all be pulling for a baseball lifer like Pedroia, but the cold hard truth is that his left knee has barred him from the majors since April 17, 2019. He may well retire before the season starts, but no one should begrudge him opting for one last shot at appearing under Fenway's bright lights instead.

YEAR	TEAM	LVL	AGE	PA	DRC+	BABIP	BRR	FRAA	WARP
2018	BOS	MLB	34	13	96	.100	-0.1	2B(3): -0.4	0.0
2019	BOS	MLB	35	21	86	.111	-0.1	2B(4): -0.2	0.0
2021 FS	BOS	MLB	37	600	96	.300	-0.5	2B -2	1.3

Hudson Potts   3B
Born: 10/28/98   Age: 22   Bats: R   Throws: R
Height: 6'3"   Weight: 218   Origin: Round 1, 2016 Draft (#24 overall)

YEAR	TEAM	LVL	AGE	PA	R	2B	3B	HR	RBI	BB	K	SB	CS	AVG/OBP/SLG
2018	LE	HI-A	19	453	66	35	1	17	58	37	112	3	1	.281/.350/.498
2018	SA	AA	19	89	5	0	0	2	5	10	33	1	0	.154/.258/.231
2019	AMA	AA	20	448	56	23	1	16	59	32	128	3	1	.227/.290/.406
2021 FS	BOS	MLB	22	600	55	23	2	16	62	37	200	2	1	.205/.263/.346

Comparables: Josh Vitters, Jonathan Villar, Matt Dominguez

Acquired for the low price of a few dozen Mitch Moreland games, Potts is a 2016 first-rounder who's perfect for the Red Sox in that he's a corner infielder who strikes out constantly. When it comes to making contact, he makes Bobby Dalbec look like Tony Gwynn.

YEAR	TEAM	LVL	AGE	PA	DRC+	BABIP	BRR	FRAA	WARP
2018	LE	HI-A	19	453	144	.348	0.3	3B(99): 0.7, 1B(8): 0.1	2.4
2018	SA	AA	19	89	43	.233	-0.2	3B(21): 0.3	-0.4
2019	AMA	AA	20	448	58	.288	-1.7	3B(86): -6.4, 2B(19): -0.7	-1.2
2021 FS	BOS	MLB	22	600	65	.288	-0.5	3B -2, 2B 0	-1.7

Jeisson Rosario CF
Born: 10/22/99   Age: 21   Bats: L   Throws: L
Height: 6'1"   Weight: 191   Origin: International Free Agent, 2016

YEAR	TEAM	LVL	AGE	PA	R	2B	3B	HR	RBI	BB	K	SB	CS	AVG/OBP/SLG
2018	FW	LO-A	18	520	79	17	5	3	34	66	107	18	12	.271/.369/.354
2019	LE	HI-A	19	525	67	14	4	3	35	87	114	11	4	.242/.372/.314
2021 FS	BOS	MLB	21	600	49	23	2	6	48	49	171	5	4	.218/.286/.307

Comparables: Billy McKinney, Daniel Fields, Anthony Gose

The main piece headed back to Boston in the Mitch Moreland trade, Rosario is a smooth operator in center field who displays plenty of patience at the plate. He's not a burner or a slugger and it's still not entirely clear he can hit, which puts his floor at Juan Lagares and his ceiling at, well, Jackie Bradley Jr.?

YEAR	TEAM	LVL	AGE	PA	DRC+	BABIP	BRR	FRAA	WARP
2018	FW	LO-A	18	520	97	.347	3.5	CF(113): -1.2, RF(1): -0.2	1.0
2019	LE	HI-A	19	525	117	.322	4.3	CF(111): 0.6, LF(5): 1.7, RF(4): 1.2	3.3
2021 FS	BOS	MLB	21	600	65	.306	0.0	CF 6, RF 0	-0.1

Connor Wong C
Born: 05/19/96   Age: 25   Bats: R   Throws: R
Height: 6'1"   Weight: 178   Origin: Round 3, 2017 Draft (#100 overall)

YEAR	TEAM	LVL	AGE	PA	R	2B	3B	HR	RBI	BB	K	SB	CS	AVG/OBP/SLG
2018	RC	HI-A	22	431	64	20	2	19	60	38	138	6	2	.269/.350/.480
2019	RC	HI-A	23	302	39	15	6	15	51	21	93	9	2	.245/.306/.507
2019	TUL	AA	23	163	17	9	1	9	31	11	50	2	1	.349/.393/.604
2021 FS	BOS	MLB	25	600	55	22	2	16	62	37	225	2	1	.203/.263/.345

Comparables: Xavier Scruggs, Carlos Moncrief, Mike Gerber

YEAR	TEAM	P. COUNT	FRM RUNS	BLK RUNS	THRW RUNS	TOT RUNS
2019	TUL	3381	-0.8	0.0	1.3	0.5
2021	BOS	16650	-4.4	-3.0	0.3	-7.2
2021	BOS	16650	-4.4	-6.5	0.3	-10.6

Acquired as part of the Mookie Betts salary dump, Wong offers an extreme power, extreme swing-and-miss profile more commonly seen in corner-infield prospects. If he can make more contact he could be a starting backstop, and if your aunt had wheels she'd be a bus.

Boston Red Sox 2021

YEAR	TEAM	LVL	AGE	PA	DRC+	BABIP	BRR	FRAA	WARP
2018	RC	HI-A	22	431	113	.372	0.9	C(71): 0.7, 2B(11): -0.5, 3B(1): -0.1	1.2
2019	RC	HI-A	23	302	101	.310	1.3	C(59): 0.7, 2B(10): 1.3, 3B(2): -0.0	1.7
2019	TUL	AA	23	163	162	.467	0.3	C(24): 0.1, 3B(10): -0.8, 2B(4): -0.2	1.5
2021 FS	BOS	MLB	25	600	64	.307	-0.4	C -11, 2B 1	-1.5

Nick Yorke 2B
Born: 04/02/02   Age: 19   Bats: R   Throws: R
Height: 6'0"   Weight: 200   Origin: Round 1, 2020 Draft (#17 overall)

The Sox were clearly trying to game the system when they popped Yorke 17th overall in the 2020 draft, as the bat-first infielder signed a deal for nearly $1 million less than slot allowance. It's not that he's a bad prospect—the former Arizona commit has impressive bat-to-ball skills and could move quickly for a prep hitter. But Yorke is a second base prospect without big power or speed and with shoulder surgery on his resume, which is why most in the draftnik community had him as a second- or third-rounder at best. Yorke's below-slot deal did free up the Sox to sign exquisitely named third-rounder Blaze Jordan, but it's fair to wonder if new GM Chaim Bloom got too cute here. We do know this much, at least: between acquiring a Jeter Downs and an N. Yorke, Bloom is very determined to troll his fanbase.

William Cuevas RHP

Born: 10/14/90 Age: 30 Bats: S Throws: R
Height: 6'2" Weight: 215 Origin:

YEAR	TEAM	LVL	AGE	W	L	SV	G	GS	IP	H	HR	BB/9	K/9	K	GB%	BABIP
2018	WOR	AAA	27	10	7	0	23	23	135[1]	120	17	2.5	8.0	121	31.2%	.272
2018	BOS	MLB	27	0	2	0	9	1	17	20	3	5.8	10.6	20	49.0%	.378
2019	KT	KBO	28	13	10	0	30	30	184	153	18	3.0	6.6	135		
2020	KT	KBO	29	10	8	0	27	27	158	152	16	2.0	6.3	110		
2021									No projection							

Comparables: Alec Mills, Austin Voth, Adam Plutko

Velocity, command and movement are the bedrocks of pitching. To hack it in the majors, you need at least two of those, and Cuevas only has the latter. A late season cameo with Boston in 2018 earned him a ring, and perhaps sensing that his big league luck could only run so much further, he repaired to Korea soon after. An extended dead arm period at the start of 2020 fluffed up his overall line, but upon his return to action in the summer, Cuevas was one of the better hurlers in the league. His pitch mix is best described as "slippery," as seemingly everything in his arsenal moves like it's covered in Crisco. When he's dealing, Korean hitters simply can't square him up. Between that and the joy he radiates in the dugout, hamming it up with teammates and goofing off whenever the camera finds him, it appears he's found his baseball home for as long as KT will have him.

YEAR	TEAM	LVL	AGE	WHIP	ERA	DRA-	WARP	MPH	FB%	WHF	CSP
2018	WOR	AAA	27	1.17	3.39	98	1.0				
2018	BOS	MLB	27	1.82	7.41	140	-0.3	92.6	39.0%	31.7%	
2019	KT	KBO	28	1.17	3.62						
2020	KT	KBO	29	1.25	4.10						
2021						No projection					

Durbin Feltman RHP

Born: 04/18/97   Age: 24   Bats: R   Throws: R
Height: 6'0"   Weight: 205   Origin: Round 3, 2018 Draft (#100 overall)

YEAR	TEAM	LVL	AGE	W	L	SV	G	GS	IP	H	HR	BB/9	K/9	K	GB%	BABIP
2018	LOW	SS	21	0	0	0	4	0	4	0	0	0.0	15.8	7	83.3%	.000
2018	GVL	LO-A	21	0	1	3	7	0	7	6	0	1.3	18.0	14	28.6%	.429
2018	SAL	HI-A	21	1	0	1	11	0	12^1	12	0	2.9	10.9	15	54.5%	.375
2019	POR	AA	22	2	3	5	43	0	51^1	42	8	5.4	9.5	54	42.6%	.268
2021 FS	BOS	MLB	24	2	3	0	57	0	50	46	8	5.3	9.3	51	40.4%	.288

Comparables: Nick Burdi, Evan Phillips, Shawn Armstrong

A once-promising reliever prospect, Feltman said he spent quarantine refining his curveball *and* his command, much like once-promising naval Captain Edward Smith focused on deck chair arrangement *and* iceberg avoidance.

YEAR	TEAM	LVL	AGE	WHIP	ERA	DRA-	WARP	MPH	FB%	WHF	CSP
2018	LOW	SS	21	0.00	0.00	28	0.2				
2018	GVL	LO-A	21	1.00	2.57	41	0.2				
2018	SAL	HI-A	21	1.30	2.19	55	0.3				
2019	POR	AA	22	1.42	5.26	105	-0.3				
2021 FS	BOS	MLB	24	1.52	4.99	115	-0.2				

Jay Groome   LHP

Born: 08/23/98   Age: 22   Bats: L   Throws: L
Height: 6'6"   Weight: 220   Origin: Round 1, 2016 Draft (#12 overall)

YEAR	TEAM	LVL	AGE	W	L	SV	G	GS	IP	H	HR	BB/9	K/9	K	GB%	BABIP
2019	RSX	ROK	20	0	0	0	2	2	2	2	0	0.0	13.5	3	80.0%	.400
2019	LOW	SS	20	0	0	0	1	1	2	3	0	4.5	13.5	3	28.6%	.429
2021 FS	BOS	MLB	22	2	3	0	57	0	50	46	8	6.1	9.3	51	45.2%	.289

Comparables: Brusdar Graterol, Carl Edwards Jr., Mat Latos

Not sure if you're an optimist or a pessimist? Ask yourself how you feel about Groome. If you're a glass-half-empty type, you can point to how the 2016 first-rounder has thrown just four official innings since the 2017 season as you notch another win for the TINSTAAPP crowd. If you tend to look on the sunnier side, you'll note that Groom is just 22, fully recovered from Tommy John surgery, and still boasts the type of stuff and workhorse frame that could make him a top-of-the-rotation starter. Young lefties who stand at 6-foot-6 and throw in the mid-90s are among the game's most coveted treasures, which is why Groome is likely to be added to the 40-man roster this offseason despite his history. If he can stay on the mound for a full season, he should skyrocket back up the prospect lists that once held him in such high regard. If not, it's tempting to say we'll all be ready to move on, but at this time next year Groome will *still* only be 23...

YEAR	TEAM	LVL	AGE	WHIP	ERA	DRA-	WARP	MPH	FB%	WHF	CSP
2019	RSX	ROK	20	1.00	0.00						
2019	LOW	SS	20	2.00	4.50	85	0.0				
2021 FS	BOS	MLB	22	1.61	5.25	119	-0.3				

Bryan Mata RHP
Born: 05/03/99 Age: 22 Bats: R Throws: R
Height: 6'3" Weight: 240 Origin: International Free Agent, 2016

YEAR	TEAM	LVL	AGE	W	L	SV	G	GS	IP	H	HR	BB/9	K/9	K	GB%	BABIP
2018	SAL	HI-A	19	6	3	0	17	17	72	58	1	7.2	7.6	61	56.6%	.297
2019	SAL	HI-A	20	3	1	0	10	10	51¹	38	1	3.2	9.1	52	64.0%	.270
2019	POR	AA	20	4	6	0	11	11	53²	54	6	4.0	9.9	59	50.3%	.350
2021 FS	BOS	MLB	22	9	9	0	26	26	150	139	19	5.2	8.2	135	46.9%	.284
2021 DC	BOS	MLB	22	1	1	0	12	3	13	12	1	5.2	8.2	12	46.9%	.284

Comparables: Sixto Sánchez, Lucas Sims, Deolis Guerra

Mata remains one of the Red Sox's best pitching prospects, but it also remains to be seen if he's particularly good. Here's what's new: Mata reportedly added a bit of velocity, hitting 98 mph at the alternate site, and he's continued to prioritize working on his two-seam fastball. Here's what's not new: his pure stuff is still lightyears ahead of his command and control, and it seems increasingly likely that he will have to find major league success out of the 'pen. Mata should get a chance to prove he belongs in the bigs at some point this season, but early results are likely to look a lot like his fastball placement: very hit or miss.

YEAR	TEAM	LVL	AGE	WHIP	ERA	DRA-	WARP	MPH	FB%	WHF	CSP
2018	SAL	HI-A	19	1.61	3.50	106	0.3				
2019	SAL	HI-A	20	1.09	1.75	75	0.8				
2019	POR	AA	20	1.45	5.03	111	-0.3				
2021 FS	BOS	MLB	22	1.50	4.79	111	0.5				
2021 DC	BOS	MLB	22	1.50	4.79	111	0.0				

Collin McHugh RHP
Born: 06/19/87 Age: 34 Bats: R Throws: R
Height: 6'2" Weight: 191 Origin: Round 18, 2008 Draft (#554 overall)

YEAR	TEAM	LVL	AGE	W	L	SV	G	GS	IP	H	HR	BB/9	K/9	K	GB%	BABIP
2018	HOU	MLB	31	6	2	0	58	0	72¹	45	6	2.6	11.7	94	34.4%	.250
2019	HOU	MLB	32	4	5	0	35	8	74²	62	12	3.6	9.9	82	39.1%	.265
2021 FS	BOS	MLB	34	10	7	0	26	26	150	133	22	3.1	9.6	159	38.4%	.286
2021 DC	BOS	MLB	34	6	4	0	44	6	64	57	9	3.1	9.6	68	38.4%	.286

Comparables: Carlos Carrasco, Garrett Richards, Jordan Zimmermann

If, like McHugh, you already had a few million dollars in the bank, would you defy public health officials to try and gut it out for the 2020 Boston Red Sox, or would you opt out, take a year off and fully rest your arm? Yeah, that's what we thought.

YEAR	TEAM	LVL	AGE	WHIP	ERA	DRA-	WARP	MPH	FB%	WHF	CSP
2018	HOU	MLB	31	0.91	1.99	60	1.9	93.6	49.6%	31.4%	
2019	HOU	MLB	32	1.23	4.70	101	0.5	92.8	33.4%	28.1%	
2021 FS	BOS	MLB	34	1.23	3.82	88	2.5	93.1	38.6%	29.2%	46.8%
2021 DC	BOS	MLB	34	1.23	3.82	88	0.9	93.1	38.6%	29.2%	46.8%

Eduardo Rodriguez LHP
Born: 04/07/93 Age: 28 Bats: L Throws: L
Height: 6'2" Weight: 231 Origin: International Free Agent, 2010

YEAR	TEAM	LVL	AGE	W	L	SV	G	GS	IP	H	HR	BB/9	K/9	K	GB%	BABIP
2018	POR	AA	25	0	0	0	2	2	8	3	0	4.5	15.8	14	69.2%	.231
2018	BOS	MLB	25	13	5	0	27	23	129^2	119	16	3.1	10.1	146	38.0%	.301
2019	BOS	MLB	26	19	6	0	34	34	203^1	195	24	3.3	9.4	213	48.2%	.318
2021 FS	BOS	MLB	28	10	7	0	26	26	150	131	16	3.4	9.9	164	44.2%	.295
2021 DC	BOS	MLB	28	8	6	0	22	22	120	105	13	3.4	9.9	132	44.2%	.295

Comparables: José Berríos, Zach Eflin, Zach Davies

In a more rational society, Rodriguez would serve as the poster child for why even the healthiest people in the world need to do their part to curb the spread of coronavirus. E-Rod missed the entire season with myocarditis—essentially inflammation of the heart—caused by COVID-19. He was not medically cleared to begin even light exercise such as walking on a treadmill until late September, and while the hope is Rodriguez will be ready to go to start the 2021 season, no one fully understands yet how athletes will or won't recover from the virus. Rodriguez is entering his final year of team control, and a productive, healthy season should leave him poised for a sizable payday. Here's hoping he's well enough to stay on the mound, and here's another plea to wear a mask, no matter how low-risk you believe yourself to be.

YEAR	TEAM	LVL	AGE	WHIP	ERA	DRA-	WARP	MPH	FB%	WHF	CSP
2018	POR	AA	25	0.88	0.00	96	0.1				
2018	BOS	MLB	25	1.26	3.82	84	2.3	95.2	51.6%	26.3%	
2019	BOS	MLB	26	1.33	3.81	91	2.9	94.9	54.3%	27.6%	
2021 FS	BOS	MLB	28	1.25	3.33	83	2.8	95.0	53.6%	27.3%	44.6%
2021 DC	BOS	MLB	28	1.25	3.33	83	2.3	95.0	53.6%	27.3%	44.6%

Chris Sale LHP

Born: 03/30/89   Age: 32   Bats: L   Throws: L
Height: 6'6"   Weight: 183   Origin: Round 1, 2010 Draft (#13 overall)

YEAR	TEAM	LVL	AGE	W	L	SV	G	GS	IP	H	HR	BB/9	K/9	K	GB%	BABIP
2018	BOS	MLB	29	12	4	0	27	27	158	102	11	1.9	13.5	237	44.0%	.283
2019	BOS	MLB	30	6	11	0	25	25	147^1	123	24	2.3	13.3	218	43.0%	.311
2021 FS	BOS	MLB	32	10	6	0	26	26	150	118	15	2.3	11.9	197	41.8%	.299
2021 DC	BOS	MLB	32	6	3	0	16	14	81.3	64	8	2.3	11.9	107	41.8%	.299

Comparables: Stephen Strasburg, Johan Santana, Pedro Martinez

For years and years the skeptics told us that Sale's wire-thin frame and unorthodox delivery would cause serious injury, and for years and years the skeptics were wrong. There's no evidence that Sale's slingshot mechanics or slight build directly led to his UCL tear, but tear it did, necessitating Tommy John surgery in late March. In truth, this was a predictable outcome for reasons beyond Sale's body or throwing motion. His average fastball velocity declined by nearly two mph between 2018 and 2019, and several trips to the IL for various arm issues offered clear foreshadowing. The good news is Sale is only set to enter his age-32 season, and many marquee pitchers have returned to form post-TJ in recent years. The suddenly cost-conscious Red Sox must be praying he can follow suit, as he is still owed $135 million over the next five seasons. For reference, you can buy nearly *two* Nate Eovaldi contracts with that much cheddar.

YEAR	TEAM	LVL	AGE	WHIP	ERA	DRA-	WARP	MPH	FB%	WHF	CSP
2018	BOS	MLB	29	0.86	2.11	50	5.6	99.1	50.1%	35.1%	
2019	BOS	MLB	30	1.09	4.40	60	4.5	96.6	46.3%	32.0%	
2021 FS	BOS	MLB	32	1.04	2.47	66	4.3	97.4	47.6%	33.0%	49.8%
2021 DC	BOS	MLB	32	1.04	2.47	66	2.4	97.4	47.6%	33.0%	49.8%

Hirokazu Sawamura 澤村 拓一   RHP

Born: 04/03/88   Age: 33   Bats: R   Throws: R
Height: 6'0"   Weight: 212   Origin:

YEAR	TEAM	LVL	AGE	W	L	SV	G	GS	IP	H	HR	BB/9	K/9	K	GB%	BABIP
2018	YOM	NPB	30	1	6	0	49	0	52¹	55	4	4.0	9.3	27		
2019	YOM	NPB	31	2	2	0	43	0	48¹	40	3	3.0	10.2	17		
2020	YOM	NPB	32	1	1	0	13		13¹	14	1	5.0	7.4	11		
2020	CHB	NPB	32	0	2	1	22		21	10	2	4.0	12.4	29		
2021 FS	BOS	MLB	33	2	2	0	57	0	50	43	6	4.3	9.2	51	41.4%	.284
2021 DC	BOS	MLB	33	2	2	0	56	0	48.7	42	6	4.3	9.2	50	41.4%	.284

Relievers are volatile. A month after making Yomiuri's Opening Day roster to start the 2020 season, Sawamura was demoted to the farm, where he lost all semblance of control before being traded to Lotte for a career up-and-down bench bat. At that point, seeking a major-league contract after the season seemed like a far-fetched dream. In two-plus months with the new team, he bounced back mightily and became one of the most dominant relievers in the Pacific League with his mid-90s fastball and devastating low-90s splitter. A potential move to the major leagues, which appears to have been his ultimate goal since his college days, doesn't seem like a farfetched idea now.

YEAR	TEAM	LVL	AGE	WHIP	ERA	DRA-	WARP	MPH	FB%	WHF	CSP
2018	YOM	NPB	30	1.57	4.64						
2019	YOM	NPB	31	1.18	2.61						
2020	YOM	NPB	32	1.65	6.08						
2020	CHB	NPB	32	0.95	1.71						
2021 FS	BOS	MLB	33	1.36	3.96	98	0.3				
2021 DC	BOS	MLB	33	1.36	3.96	98	0.3				

Boston Red Sox 2021

Connor Seabold RHP
Born: 01/24/96   Age: 25   Bats: R   Throws: R
Height: 6'2"   Weight: 190   Origin: Round 3, 2017 Draft (#83 overall)

YEAR	TEAM	LVL	AGE	W	L	SV	G	GS	IP	H	HR	BB/9	K/9	K	GB%	BABIP
2018	CLR	HI-A	22	4	4	0	12	12	71^2	57	6	1.8	8.5	68	46.5%	.262
2018	REA	AA	22	1	4	0	11	11	58^2	55	10	2.9	9.8	64	34.5%	.292
2019	PHE	ROK	23	0	1	0	1	1	2^1	6	0	0.0	7.7	2	54.5%	.545
2019	PHW	ROK	23	0	0	0	2	2	5	1	0	0.0	18.0	10	83.3%	.167
2019	CLR	HI-A	23	1	0	0	2	1	9	4	1	1.0	10.0	10	50.0%	.158
2019	REA	AA	23	3	1	0	7	7	40	35	2	2.2	8.1	36	45.5%	.303
2021 FS	BOS	MLB	25	2	2	0	57	0	50	46	7	3.2	8.5	47	39.5%	.285
2021 DC	BOS	MLB	25	0	0	0	3	3	13.7	12	1	3.2	8.5	13	39.5%	.285

Comparables: Marco Gonzales, Ryan Helsley, Tyler Wilson

Former Phillies farmhand Connor Seabold has the name of a man destined for Boston and the arsenal of one who's likely to spend some time in Pawtucket. There's no. 4 starter upside here, but a floor that suggests he should start studying South Station train schedules.

YEAR	TEAM	LVL	AGE	WHIP	ERA	DRA-	WARP	MPH	FB%	WHF	CSP
2018	CLR	HI-A	22	0.99	3.77	68	1.7				
2018	REA	AA	22	1.26	4.91	74	1.2				
2019	PHE	ROK	23	2.57	11.57						
2019	PHW	ROK	23	0.20	0.00						
2019	CLR	HI-A	23	0.56	1.00	58	0.2				
2019	REA	AA	23	1.12	2.25	84	0.4				
2021 FS	BOS	MLB	25	1.28	3.80	94	0.4				
2021 DC	BOS	MLB	25	1.28	3.80	94	0.2				

Noah Song RHP
Born: 05/28/97   Age: 24   Bats: R   Throws: R
Height: 6'4"   Weight: 200   Origin: Round 4, 2019 Draft (#137 overall)

YEAR	TEAM	LVL	AGE	W	L	SV	G	GS	IP	H	HR	BB/9	K/9	K	GB%	BABIP
2019	LOW	SS	22	0	0	0	7	7	17	10	0	2.6	10.1	19	41.5%	.244
2021 FS	BOS	MLB	24	2	3	0	57	0	50	47	7	4.9	7.9	44	37.9%	.282

Comparables: Jesse Hahn, Hayden Penn, Josh Zeid

The U.S. Navy ruled that Song must put his duty to his nation above his duty to Red Sox Nation; they ordered the Naval Academy grad to report to flight school at Naval Air Station Pensacola last June. He could apply for early release again this spring, but it seems Song is going to spend the next few years focused on an entirely different type of launch angle.

YEAR	TEAM	LVL	AGE	WHIP	ERA	DRA-	WARP	MPH	FB%	WHF	CSP
2019	LOW	SS	22	0.88	1.06	51	0.5				
2021 FS	BOS	MLB	24	1.50	4.84	115	-0.2				

Josh Taylor LHP
Born: 03/02/93   Age: 28   Bats: L   Throws: L
Height: 6'5"   Weight: 245   Origin: Undrafted Free Agent, 2014

YEAR	TEAM	LVL	AGE	W	L	SV	G	GS	IP	H	HR	BB/9	K/9	K	GB%	BABIP
2018	VIS	HI-A	25	1	2	5	14	0	16	16	1	2.8	11.2	20	42.9%	.366
2018	POR	AA	25	2	5	8	33	0	35²	42	1	4.5	9.3	37	50.9%	.383
2019	WOR	AAA	26	1	1	3	20	0	23¹	18	2	4.2	12.3	32	47.2%	.320
2019	BOS	MLB	26	2	2	0	52	1	47¹	40	5	3.0	11.8	62	44.7%	.321
2020	BOS	MLB	27	1	1	0	8	0	7¹	7	2	6.1	8.6	7	43.5%	.238
2021 FS	BOS	MLB	28	2	2	0	57	0	50	43	5	3.9	9.9	54	46.1%	.292
2021 DC	BOS	MLB	28	2	2	0	42	0	36.3	31	4	3.9	9.9	40	46.1%	.292

Comparables: Ashton Goudeau, Andrew Suárez, Spencer Turnbull

This was a trying year by anyone's standards, but Taylor had it particularly rough. He was among the bevy of Red Sox southpaws to test positive for COVID-19 in early July, which kept him on the IL until mid-August. When Taylor returned he was ineffectively wild across eight disastrous games before shoulder tendonitis ended his season. Assuming he recovers fully from both ailments, Taylor can still serve as one of Boston's primary lefty relievers, bolstered by his Great Stuff(TM) but hampered by, well, let's be charitable and go with "inconsistent" control. But there are lots of arms in Boston's pen with similar profiles, and it's a shame Taylor was denied a real chance at separating himself from the pack.

YEAR	TEAM	LVL	AGE	WHIP	ERA	DRA-	WARP	MPH	FB%	WHF	CSP
2018	VIS	HI-A	25	1.31	2.81	51	0.4				
2018	POR	AA	25	1.68	3.79	80	0.5				
2019	WOR	AAA	26	1.24	2.70	60	0.7				
2019	BOS	MLB	26	1.18	3.04	80	0.7	96.2	60.1%	33.7%	
2020	BOS	MLB	27	1.64	9.82	104	0.1	94.8	52.1%	28.4%	
2021 FS	BOS	MLB	28	1.30	3.57	88	0.6	95.9	58.4%	32.5%	43.5%
2021 DC	BOS	MLB	28	1.30	3.57	88	0.4	95.9	58.4%	32.5%	43.5%

Thad Ward RHP
Born: 01/16/97 Age: 24 Bats: R Throws: R
Height: 6'3" Weight: 182 Origin: Round 5, 2018 Draft (#160 overall)

YEAR	TEAM	LVL	AGE	W	L	SV	G	GS	IP	H	HR	BB/9	K/9	K	GB%	BABIP
2018	LOW	SS	21	0	3	0	11	11	31	33	2	3.5	7.8	27	54.3%	.337
2019	GVL	LO-A	22	5	2	0	13	13	72¹	51	2	3.1	10.8	87	47.8%	.280
2019	SAL	HI-A	22	3	3	0	12	12	54	38	4	5.3	11.7	70	47.1%	.296
2021 FS	BOS	MLB	24	2	3	0	57	0	50	46	7	5.6	9.0	49	43.7%	.287

Comparables: Albert Abreu, Justin Grimm, Tyler Thornburg

Ward remains one of Boston's more intriguing pitching prospects, which is why it's notable that he never got the call up from Ft. Myers to join the Sox's alternate site in Pawtucket. Or, put another way, the Sox denied Thad Ward a shot to serve as a ward, which seems more than a thad bit odd.

YEAR	TEAM	LVL	AGE	WHIP	ERA	DRA-	WARP	MPH	FB%	WHF	CSP
2018	LOW	SS	21	1.45	3.77	159	-0.8				
2019	GVL	LO-A	22	1.05	1.99	66	1.7				
2019	SAL	HI-A	22	1.30	2.33	89	0.5				
2021 FS	BOS	MLB	24	1.56	5.16	116	-0.2				

Garrett Whitlock RHP
Born: 06/11/96 Age: 25 Bats: R Throws: R
Height: 6'5" Weight: 190 Origin: Round 18, 2017 Draft (#542 overall)

YEAR	TEAM	LVL	AGE	W	L	SV	G	GS	IP	H	HR	BB/9	K/9	K	GB%	BABIP
2018	CSC	LO-A	22	2	2	0	7	7	40	23	1	1.6	9.9	44	61.1%	.239
2018	TAM	HI-A	22	5	3	0	14	13	70	60	2	3.5	9.5	74	50.8%	.310
2018	TRN	AA	22	1	0	0	2	1	10²	10	0	5.9	3.4	4	55.9%	.294
2019	TRN	AA	23	3	3	0	14	14	70¹	73	4	2.3	7.3	57	55.5%	.322
2021 FS	BOS	MLB	25	2	2	0	57	0	50	46	6	3.7	7.7	42	50.3%	.280
2021 DC	BOS	MLB	25	1	1	0	36	0	24.3	22	3	3.7	7.7	20	50.3%	.280

Comparables: Taylor Rogers, Kyle McGowin, Ramón Rosso

Swiped from the Yankees with the fourth pick in the Rule 5 draft, Whitlock is a big right-hander who's still recovering from July 2019 Tommy John surgery. He should be ready for spring training and has a modicum of upside, which arguably already makes him one of the Red Sox's better relievers.

YEAR	TEAM	LVL	AGE	WHIP	ERA	DRA-	WARP	MPH	FB%	WHF	CSP
2018	CSC	LO-A	22	0.75	1.12	76	0.7				
2018	TAM	HI-A	22	1.24	2.44	82	1.1				
2018	TRN	AA	22	1.59	0.84	115	0.0				
2019	TRN	AA	23	1.29	3.07	107	-0.2				
2021 FS	BOS	MLB	25	1.34	3.93	96	0.3				
2021 DC	BOS	MLB	25	1.34	3.93	96	0.2				

Red Sox Prospects

The State of the System:
The Red Sox system continues to improve, but it's more depth than top-end talent at present.

The Top Ten:

─────── ★ ★ ★ *2021 Top 101 Prospect* **#85** ★ ★ ★ ───────

1 **Triston Casas** 3B   OFP: 60   ETA: Late 2022/Early 2023
Born: 01/15/00   Age: 21   Bats: L   Throws: R   Height: 6'4"   Weight: 238
Origin: Round 1, 2018 Draft (#26 overall)

The Report: As a first-round prep first baseman, you'd expect Casas to have a big offensive projection. He does. The hit tool isn't quite as good as the elite cold-corner prospects, but Casas generates a lot of pop without a lot of length and approach improvements could get the hit tool to above-average. He played some third base in high school, but has solely played first in the pros, and while he should end up more than passable there, some defensive refinement will be necessary as the game speed increases up the organizational ladder. Even in his first pro season in 2019—and given a challenging full-season assignment—Casas showed improvements as the season wore on. So there could be a breakout looming once we all get back to a more normal minor league season.

Development Track: I have a pet theory that the prospects hit hardest by the lack of a 2020 campaign were young, high-ceiling prospects with one year in A-ball. Now this isn't based on anything scientific, and frankly the two major points of improvement we'd look for in games here—approach and defense—got positive reviews on the alternate site side. Would I be more confident Casas will hit enough to carry the first base profile if he did it in the Carolina League? Sure. But he's on the right track. We also got good reports on the power, but you already knew he'd crush dingers. We'll still have to wait another year for the potential breakout, but we've had to wait another year for a lot of things.

Variance: High. There are thin margins for the prep first base profile, so you'd like to see a long track record of mashing in the pros. Casas doesn't have that yet.

Mark Barry's Fantasy Take: Casas has emerged as one of the most "I Once Caught a Fish THIS Big" guys from alternative site reports, with tales of his raw power and newly developed physique growing more extravagant with each retelling. The ceiling feels Pete Alonso-ish, but the realistic outcome might come more in the Mitch Moreland aisle. Still good, but less exciting.

2. Jeter Downs   SS   OFP: 60   ETA: Late 2021 maybe, likely 2022
Born: 07/27/98   Age: 22   Bats: R   Throws: R   Height: 5'11"   Weight: 195
Origin: Round 1, 2017 Draft (#32 overall)

The Report: When the 32nd-overall pick bounces between three teams in four years after being selected, you do tend to wonder why a high draft pick would be traded that much. In the case of Downs, there is some debate where he ends up defensively and just how high the ceiling might be. Given his involvement in the Mookie Betts deal, the Red Sox seem to view his upside as quite high, especially with the bat. He has a naturally aggressive approach, but has shown an improved ability to be more selective at the plate and use the entire field. Downs isn't the fastest guy by the stopwatch, but has good instincts that help both his infield range and ability to steal bases.

Development Track: A highly touted high school shortstop making it to Double-A in his second full season of pro ball is very noteworthy, regardless of how many organizations he's been with. The original plan for 2020 was to continue his rapid matriculation while getting accustomed to yet another set of coaches and philosophies. By every estimation the development track continues upward with the likelihood he switches over to second base in 2021, making stops in Triple-A and a potential big-league call-up not out of the question.

Variance: High. It's no small feat having to listen to three sets of voices over three years. No one would fault him for some amount of stagnation as a result, but his success so far is very much to his credit.

Mark Barry's Fantasy Take: Huge Jeter Downs guy here. We're looking at an above-average hit tool paired with the ability to work walks and a knack for base thievery, not to mention enough power to the pull side to potentially turn into a 20/20 guy at the six. He's a top-50 dynasty guy for me and honestly, I think I prefer him to Casas in fantasy.

3. Noah Song   RHP   OFP: 55   ETA: Around a year after his service commitment ends.
Born: 05/28/97   Age: 24   Bats: R   Throws: R   Height: 6'4"   Weight: 200
Origin: Round 4, 2019 Draft (#137 overall)

The Report: If Song had been allowed to transfer to the Navy Reserve after graduating, he'd be a Top 101 prospect. He's a four-pitch, advanced college arm of similar quality to the pitchers who rank around the middle of the 101 in any given year, and in some alternate world would've moved very quickly and been at the forefront of Boston's rebuild. Of course, the Red Sox never would've been able to take him as a below-slot fourth-rounder without the availability questions…

Development Track: Song would not have pitched in 2020 even if there were a season; he reported to naval flight school in June after he was denied a deferral waiver. He's eligible for early release from his service commitment as early as May 2021, but our sources with the Red Sox were unsure when he'd be able to resume his professional career, and the Secretary of Defense who was making these calls got fired by tweet last week. Song pitching in the 2021 Olympics makes way too much sense for everyone involved for it not to happen, not that political decisions are always based on making sense or anything.

Variance: High. On talent, he's better than this, but it's a unique level of uncertainty here. We would note, though, that many prospects ended up having a lost 2020 not all that unlike Song, so if he ends up pitching in 2021 he might not be as far behind the curve as you'd think.

Mark Barry's Fantasy Take: Before getting into the Song-of-it-all, I just wanted to reemphasize the majesty of this sentence:

> "our sources with the Red Sox were unsure when he'd be able to resume his professional career, and the Secretary of Defense who was making these calls just got fired by tweet last week"

Anyway, there are a lot of questions surrounding Song's reemergence onto the prospect scene, but funny enough, lost development isn't really one of them, thanks to, uh, a global pandemic that kept all minor leaguers out of competitive games. Song was fairly advanced before his Naval service, so it's easy to envision the Red Sox moving him pretty quickly when he gets back in the fold. Still, I don't think you'd have to be too aggressive with him outside of leagues that roster 250+ prospects.

4

Jarren Duran   OF   OFP: 55   ETA: 2022, could force his way into 2021 discussion
Born: 09/05/96   Age: 24   Bats: L   Throws: R   Height: 6'2"   Weight: 187
Origin: Round 7, 2018 Draft (#220 overall)

The Report: You might not find another player in this system who invokes as wide a range of opinions. Finding a seventh-rounder who can potentially bring value to the major-league club is always a feather in the cap for the scouting department, no matter if he's a bench bat, defensive/baserunning sub, everyday guy, or star player. All are potential future outcomes for Duran, depending on whom you talk to. After playing the infield in college, he is adapting to life in the outfield where his plus-plus speed plays well in the gaps, even as his reads and angles improve with more reps at the new position. That speed is evident on the basepaths as well, as he uses it to his advantage to get on-base with his slap-contact approach. The power is still under development as he's adjusting to drive the ball more with authority to the pull-side.

Development Track: Duran burst onto the scene surpassing every expectation in his two seasons since being drafted. However, the buzzsaw who had carved up the lower levels met some resistance in Double-A and again in the 2019 Fall League against better competition. Reports from the Pawtucket alternate training site suggest he had acclimated to the environment and addressed many of the concerns associated with his profile. Progressing to a well-rounded hitter, with the raw athletic tools he possesses, puts him in line to be patrolling the Fenway outfield within the next year.

Variance: High. Simply because of the multitude of different opinions we received from scouts and front office types.

Mark Barry's Fantasy Take: Duran is very, very fast. And rumor has it that he got more compact with his swing, enabling him to lift more balls in the air. Had that development happened in actual games (and if it's real, I guess), he'd probably be garnering a lot more buzz in fantasy circles. The speed alone has him flirting with the top-100 with room for more if he can somehow muster 10-15 homers.

5   Bryan Mata   RHP   OFP: 55   ETA: 2021
Born: 05/03/99   Age: 22   Bats: R   Throws: R   Height: 6'3"   Weight: 240
Origin: International Free Agent, 2016

The Report: Consistently praised by Red Sox brass throughout the minor league-less summer, Mata's body is finally maturing to match the big-time stuff he showed off as one of the youngest players in each of his stateside seasons. Always known as a hard thrower with fastball velocities in the mid-to-upper 90s, the issue was his ability to throw quality strikes given how much movement he generates on each of his pitches. Those within the org believe he has simplified his delivery which has allowed for more consistency locating the heater. He's also added a cutter that flashes plus. Paired with a curveball and change that are both at least average, the difference between being a frontline starter or perhaps back-end of the rotation type will wholly depend on keeping the walk rate down.

Development Track: Given the myriad directions a player of this type could go development-wise, Mata appears to be one of the few who has made substantial gains this year. Listed last year at 160 pounds, he's now well over 200 on a nearly filled out athletic frame. With the physical growth here instead of projected, maintaining his newly tweaked mechanics will be the cornerstone of his early 2021 focus.

Variance: Extreme. The news has all been positive regarding Mata, but two things stick out: 1) big physical gains can sometimes be troublesome for a pitcher's arm, and 2) once you've earned a reputation as a "thrower" with control issues, it's awfully hard to turn that around completely.

Mark Barry's Fantasy Take: If you like speculating for saves, in the minor leagues, then Mata could be your guy. If he stays in the rotation, though, you're looking at a right-handed Martín Pérez, which is extremely Not What You Want.

6 Bobby Dalbec 3B OFP: 55 ETA: Debuted in 2020
Born: 06/29/95   Age: 26   Bats: R   Throws: R   Height: 6'4"   Weight: 227
Origin: Round 4, 2016 Draft (#118 overall)

The Report: This will be Dalbec's fifth and final appearance on a Red Sox prospect list, and if we're honest, he hasn't changed a whole heckuva lot over the years. Now, it's been a good development track. There were quite a few outcomes where the swing-and-miss ate into his performance too much in the upper minors, while others saw him try his luck as a pitcher at 25 after another season hitting .220 in Portland. But his TTO style worked all the way up the ladder, and he even cut the Ks enough in 2019 where you could see enough of the power playing in games to make the profile work as an everyday player.

Development Track: He got his major-league shot in 2020 after the Red Sox sent Mitch Moreland to San Diego, and you got the full Bobby Dalbec experience. He hit a home run every 11.5 plate appearances, and struck out every 2.4 plate appearances. He's unlikely to sustain the former—although it's 30-home-run pop—and will need to improve the latter. It's not an approach issue, as he continues to rack up the free passes, but his in-zone contact rate was only a smidge better than Jo Adell's (that's bad). The overall line was buoyed by a .394 BABIP, and the profile remains quite boom-or-bust. He played mostly first base in deference to Rafael Devers, but that might get flipped soon, despite my remaining bullish on Devers' glove.

Variance: Medium. Yes, Dalbec made the majors and hit a bunch of dingers, but that batting average could end up closer to .220 than .260, and then the whole profile looks more like a bench bat.

Mark Barry's Fantasy Take: Pretty much every sample size was small this season, but only Jorge Alfaro and Luis Robert swung and missed more frequently than Dalbec this season. The Red Sox rookie also struck out more than 40 percent of the time. It's possible you could get a .260 average and a bunch of dingers from Dalbec (like you did this year), but that's like the absolute 90th percentile outcome if he's going to whiff this much. You're more likely looking at a batting average flirting with the Mendoza Line, at which point not even solid plate discipline will get him on base enough to be useful outside of the power department.

7. Nick Yorke 2B   OFP: 55   ETA: 2024
Born: 04/02/02   Age: 19   Bats: R   Throws: R   Height: 6'0"   Weight: 200
Origin: Round 1, 2020 Draft (#17 overall)

The Report: No player selected in the first round of this year's draft caused more head-scratching than the 17th-overall selection by Boston. An Arizona commit who seemed destined to make it onto campus because of his defensive limitations and overall athletic profile, the Sox believed he was the best hitter in the class without exception. Losing their second-round pick due to the sign-stealing scandal, they feared he wouldn't make it to their next pick at 89 and didn't want to leave it to chance. While puzzling at the time, Yorke demonstrated his advanced hit tool at the alternate training site, often facing grown men many years ahead of him in their development while still managing to compete. Likely destined for second base as a fringe-average defender, the term "carrying tool" has never been more applicable than it is here in reference to the offensive potential moving forward.

Development Track: As one of the youngest players at ANY alternate site this year, Yorke held his own. His development arc is still gauged in years despite the promising early signs, and he needs to shore up any and all defensive concerns that exist. Additionally, while all the talk has been about the bat—and rightfully so—there is still the need to grow into power which evaluators believe will eventually come thanks to a smooth stroke that creates natural loft. Look for him to follow a similar path to that of Casas.

Variance: Extreme. When you're known exceptionally for one thing, you better find other ways to diversify your toolset, lest you lose that defining quality, leaving you with nothing else to offer.

Mark Barry's Fantasy Take: Between Yorke likely being 2B-only and lacking much pop in the stick, he's a deep-league MI candidate or AL-only guy. Otherwise, he doesn't need to be on the radar right now.

8. Matthew Lugo SS   OFP: 55   ETA: Late 2023 or 2024
Born: 05/09/01   Age: 20   Bats: R   Throws: R   Height: 6'1"   Weight: 185
Origin: Round 2, 2019 Draft (#69 overall)

The Report: Lugo was a physically projectable shortstop who was young for his draft class. In his first pro summer he displayed a broad base of skills, but perhaps lacked a standout tool. He also looked a bit overmatched at the plate in his brief Penn League cameo against more experienced arms. It wasn't hard to see the outline of a solid everyday shortstop, though.

Development Track: Lugo has added some good, lean muscle to his frame and he already showed solid pull-side raw power. He hasn't given back the above-average speed or range at shortstop, but the glove remains ahead of the bat developmentally. All in all though, there continue to be positive markers on his offensive projection, and he will still be a teenager to start the 2021 season.

Variance: Extreme. The physical growth is a plus and the added power potential adds to the upside, but we are still talking about a 19-year-old who has played two games outside of the complex.

Mark Barry's Fantasy Take: Lugo's tools standing toe-to-toe in the ring, exhausted.

Plus speed *Crowd erupts "Yaaay"

Not much present power *Crowd erupts "Booooo"

Adding muscle, flashing pull-side pop "Yaaay"

No experience against advanced competition (and middling success in Complex League) "Booooo"

Projectable teenager "Yaaay", good mechanics "Yaaay", Potential for 4.5 category contribution "Yaaay".

9 Gilberto Jimenez   CF   OFP: 50   ETA: 2023
Born: 07/08/00   Age: 20   Bats: S   Throws: R   Height: 5'11"   Weight: 160
Origin: International Free Agent, 2017

The Report: Despite a meager five-figure bonus, Jimenez developed quickly with the lumber and was one of the best pure bat-to-ball guys in the New York-Penn League in 2019. The pure contact ability is easy plus, but there isn't much raw pop and the bat speed is fringy. He has the burn part of slash-and-burn down as he's a plus runner and aggressive on the bases. Jimenez should stick in center due to his foot speed and instincts although the arm is on the fringy side. He may have limited offensive upside due to the combination of a lack of physicality and an aggressive approach at the plate, but he's going to be a scout's favorite because of everything else.

Development Track: Jimenez should start 2021 in A-ball and the bat shouldn't really be challenged until Double-A.

Variance: High. The hit tool might be plus, but it's going to need to be, and we haven't seen it against better velocity or sequencing yet.

Mark Barry's Fantasy Take: This is the kind of guy who I think might be affected most by the lack of reps in 2020, unfortunately. He has tools (ie: those sweet, sweet wheels) and makes a ton of contact, but does lack experience. There's enough current promise to keep an eye on him, but I don't think you need to run out and make an immediate acquisition.

10 Tanner Houck   RHP   OFP: 50   ETA: Debuted in 2020
Born: 06/29/96   Age: 25   Bats: R   Throws: R   Height: 6'5"   Weight: 230
Origin: Round 1, 2017 Draft (#24 overall)

The Report: Houck transitioned to the pen in 2019, but the Red Sox stretched him back out and used him as a starter for the big club towards the end of 2020. He still primarily deploys a sinker/slider mix. The fastball can hit the mid-90s in short bursts, but was more 91-94 as a starter. It has heavy sink with some run as well, but Houck can be a bit loose with his command of the pitch and will get erratic with his control as well. The slider is a big breaker in the low 80s. It can tend to have more sweep than depth, but there's enough two-plane action here to miss bats. Houck also throws the occasional split-change which doesn't really have enough velo, separation, or sink at present to even keep lefties honest.

Development Track: Houck was nothing short of dominant in his three starts for the 2020 Red Sox, but over the long haul the stuff and command might not be enough to stick in a rotation (the 2021 Red Sox rotation will give him plenty of opportunities, though). It's a good enough two-pitch combo to work in the seventh and eighth inning, although given his platoon issues over the years, he may need to deployed strategically.

Variance: Low. Houck looked more than ready to get major-league hitters out in his three start cameo. The lack of a weapon against lefties might limit him to the bullpen or some to a role as some sort of bulk guy role where you can leverage a plus two-pitch mix, but he's an asset to your pitching staff in 2021.

Mark Barry's Fantasy Take: I'd be a lot more interested in Houck if his splitter were more developed, as he was actually really good in a brief stint in Boston toward the end of the 2020 season. As it stands, though, he's probably a reliever, and not really a high-leverage one at that.

The Prospects You Meet Outside The Top Ten:

Solid pitching prospects, but limited upside

Thad Ward RHP Born: 01/16/97 Age: 24 Bats: R Throws: R Height: 6'3" Weight: 182 Origin: Round 5, 2018 Draft (#160 overall)

Ward isn't a markedly different pitcher now compared to when he ranked fifth in the system last year. There's just been improvement around him. He's more likely to stick as a starter than Houck, given the more rounded out arsenal with a plus slider/cutter and two other useable secondaries. Ward also has less experience as a starter—he was more of a multi-inning reliever at Central Florida—and the frame is on the slender side. There's a fourth starter projection, but he's a bit further away than Houck, and there's a little less upside than Mata and Murphy. So he slides out of the top ten this year. But there really isn't a significant difference from 7 to 15 in this system.

Connor Seabold RHP Born: 01/24/96 Age: 25 Bats: R Throws: R Height: 6'2" Weight: 190 Origin: Round 3, 2017 Draft (#83 overall)

A third-round pick for the Phillies in 2017, the Phillies sent Seabold (and Nick Pivetta) to Boston for Brandon Workman and Heath Hembree. Seabold is not overpowering; his fastball will touch the mid 90s, but sits lower. Seabold has three secondary pitches in a slider, curveball, and changeup, with his changeup the best of the bunch. He has above-average command and a good feel for pitching, making him a major-league-ready back-end starter. He has a strong enough foundation that he could take another step forward if any of his pitches makes an improvement.

Chris Murphy LHP Born: 06/05/98 Age: 23 Bats: L Throws: L Height: 6'1" Weight: 175 Origin: Round 6, 2019 Draft (#197 overall)
Despite putting up gaudy strikeout numbers in college, Murphy put up equally bad walk totals as well, relegating him to the sixth round of the 2019 draft. It didn't take long for coaches to make adjustments to the delivery which not only cleared a path for more control, but also upped the velocity by a full grade. Now up to 95 with a four-pitch mix, Murphy knows how to get batters out with regularity and could move quickly up the system.

Good upside, but a ways away

Chih-Jung Liu RHP Born: 04/07/99 Age: 22 Bats: S Throws: R Height: 6'0" Weight: 185 Origin: International Free Agent, 2019
Signed out of Taiwan with a fastball reaching triple digits, Liu is still getting accustomed to life half a world away. While getting on a throwing program and training regimen traditional to major league orgs, Liu has worked on finishing his secondary pitches more consistently as the velocity hasn't quite flashed where it was when he was signed.

Bradley Blalock RHP Born: 12/25/00 Age: 20 Bats: R Throws: R Height: 6'2" Weight: 190 Origin: Round 32, 2019 Draft (#977 overall)
A relative unknown when selected late in the 2019 draft out of high school, Blalock impressed at instructs showing a four-pitch mix, projectable body, not to mention a heater that sat 94-95 with riding life. He's a long ways away, but it's easy to dream on this kind of player.

Interesting Draft Follow

Blaze Jordan 3B Born: 12/19/02 Age: 18 Bats: R Throws: R Height: 6'2" Weight: 220 Origin: Round 3, 2020 Draft (#89 overall)
[extreme Southie voice] Blays hits balls wicked fah. We've seen this kind of player make headlines ever since Bryce Harper peppered the back wall of Tropicana Field at a high school showcase. Truth is, next to none present the total package anywhere remotely near where Harper was as a prep. On the plus side, Jordan is on the young side for his class, and his hit tool might be closer to average with his ability to make hard contact.

Jeremy Wu-Yelland Born: 06/24/99 Age: 22 Bats: L Throws: L Height: 6'2" Weight: 210 Origin: Round 4, 2020 Draft (#118 overall)

Part of Boston's draft strategy was leveraging under-slot deals (like Wu-Yelland) into higher priced, over-slot players in an effort to acquire higher ceiling talent. A southpaw with a funky delivery, Wu-Yelland had been relegated to almost exclusively coming out of the pen because of the mechanics. That funk plays up as a reliever, with radar readings at instructs ticking up to 97. So even though he may have been seen as an afterthought at draft time, the makings of a future dynamic reliever are in play.

You were going to ask about him in the comments

Jay Groome   LHP   Born: 08/23/98   Age: 22   Bats: L   Throws: L   Height: 6'6"   Weight: 220   Origin: Round 1, 2016 Draft (#12 overall)

Groome was finally back to full health in 2020. He looked fine at the alternate site—Boston was one of the teams which broadcast a lot of its action, so we've got a lot more video on Groome than for other prospects this year. Back when he was the 12th-overall pick in 2016, Groome's projection was enormous; he was one of the best prep pitching prospects I've ever seen. After years of arm injuries, there's still pieces of it here, but we're just not talking about a potential future ace anymore. The curveball still flashes but it's no longer a 70 projection, and the fastball and command haven't ended up getting all the way there either. His falling off the list is more due to the system getting much stronger around him, but we're talking about a mid-rotation or bullpen prospect with an injury history now, not a potential future ace.

Top Talents 25 and Under (as of 4/1/2021):

1. Rafael Devers, 3B
2. Alex Verdugo, OF
3. Triston Casas, 1B
4. Jeter Downs, SS
5. Noah Song, RHPF
6. Jarren Duran, OF
7. Bryan Mata, RHP
8. Bobby Dalbec, 3B
9. Nick Yorke, 2B
10. Michael Chavis, 1B

Rafael Devers had a down 2020 coming off a 2019 in which he got MVP votes. Offensively, he more or less just lost 50 points of average, and that type of thing happens over a short season. He did crater defensively, and that's not great considering his obvious spot to slide to is first base, the home of the best prospect in the system. Wherever he ends up over the long haul, we expect him to put up more 2019-quality seasons in the years ahead.

Alex Verdugo is not Mookie Betts. He will never be Mookie Betts. But if you're evaluating Verdugo solely on his individual on-the-field merits, he's still on the same track as when he was a top 25 prospect in baseball a few years ago. He hit .302 this year, and that's probably for real; we've long pegged him as a plus-plus hit tool type. He should be a good player on the next good Boston team.

Michael Chavis didn't hit at all this year, managing just a 70 DRC+. He's got some positional versatility—he played second and outfield in addition to first this year—but he's not hitting as much in the majors as we projected. He might be settling in as more of a utility type or second-division regular.

Darwinzon Hernandez missed most of this year with shoulder issues. The Red Sox have toyed with converting him back to starting, and if we had any confidence he could pull it off he'd have certainly made the list. Considering him as a reliever, he's a bit off the bottom in an improved system.

Part 3: Featured Articles

Red Sox All-Time Top 10 Players

by Rob Mains

POSITION PLAYERS

BOBBY DOERR, 2B (1937–1951)
Pedroia was the best, but Doer wasn't not far behind. He hit .288/.362/.461 in 14 seasons, playing at least 132 games in all but his first and last seasons, and 1944-45 in the military. He had power for a second baseman, hitting 15 or more homers ten straight years, driving in 100 runs six times out of, usually, the no. 5 spot in the lineup. He's the only Red Sox player to hit for the cycle twice and was well-regarded for his defense as well.

DUSTIN PEDROIA, 2B (2006–2019)
On August 1, 2017, Pedroia went on the injured list with the knee injury that would ultimately cut his career short. To that point, he had a .301/.367/.443 batting line over nearly 1,483 games and was on a Hall of Fame trajectory. He was Rookie of the Year in 2007 and MVP the next year, leading the league with 213 hits, 118 runs, and 54 doubles, winning the first of his four career Gold Gloves. He's the best-hitting second baseman in club history. Both he and Doerr were expert at taking advantage of Fenway Park, but Pedroia holds the edge in neutral parks.

WADE BOGGS, 3B (1982–1992)
He led the league in batting five times and on-base percentage six times while in Boston. He .338 average and .428 on-base percentage are second only to Williams in franchise history. His batting skills and gap power (he hit 40 or more doubles seven straight years) resulted in Boggs leading the league in intentional walks every year from 1987 to 1992. Because the Red Sox were going through a particularly benighted period as Boggs was coming up, they made him repeat

each level despite his hitting a consistent .300-plus from age 19 on. He didn't get regular at-bats until he was 25, and in some senses it was a close thing that his career happened at all.

NOMAR GARCIAPARRA, SS (1996–2004)
He's the reason Pedroia and Doerr can't claim the title of best-hitting middle infielder in Sox history. Garciaparra hit .323/.370/.553 with Boston, batting over .300 in all but his injury-shortened 2001 season. He won back-to-back batting titles in 1999 and 2000, hitting .357 and .372. He's the only shortstop to lead the league in intentional walks, drawing 20 in 2000. Known for his elaborate pre-at bat ritual, he was Boston's Moses—he helped lead the team, 78-84 in his rookie season, to three postseason appearances, but dealt away at the 2004 trade deadline, missed out on the franchise's first World Championship since 1918.

TRIS SPEAKER, OF (1907–1915)
The Chalmers Award, named for a car company (corporate sponsorships aren't a new thing), was the first MVP Award, and Speaker was Boston's first winner, garnering the trophy in 1912 for hitting .383/.464/.567, leading the league with 53 doubles and 10 homers while playing an outstanding center field. He was the team's best hitter on its World Champion teams of 1912 and 1915. After he held out before the 1916 season rather than accept a pay cut from $18,000 to $9,000—this was after he hit .322/.416/.411—he was traded to Cleveland, kicking off a tradition of shipping Hall of Famer outfielders away from Boston for financial reasons.

TED WILLIAMS, OF (1939–1960)
The best player in baseball today is Mike Trout. Trout has never had a season in which he's matched Williams' career averages of a .344 batting average, .482 on-base percentage (highest in history), or .634 slugging percentage. Williams led the league in runs, homers, and RBI four times, slugging nine times, and on-base twelve times. And he did this while missing five years for military service. He was a complicated man, not always easy to like, but his hitting ability was always easy to love.

CARL YASTRZEMSKI, OF (1961–1983)
The Red Sox had quite a run of left fielders. His Triple Crown year of 1967, when he also led he league in runs, hits, total bases, on-base, and slugging, during the Deadball Era II, was one of the most remarkable offensive seasons in the majors since Williams retired. He holds the franchise records for games, plate appearances, runs, and RBI and is even fourth in stolen bases.

DWIGHT EVANS, OF (1972–1990)

The durable right fielder with the cannon arm played 140 or more games 11 times in his Red Sox career. He had outstanding on-base skills, with a career on-base percentage (.369) nearly 100 points higher than his batting average (.272). And he had pop in his bat, hitting 20 or more home runs 11 times and 24 or more doubles 12 times. Only Yastrzemski played more games for the team. Evans spent more time batting second in the order than he did at any other lineup position, a quietly revolutionary act that was missed at the time.

JIM RICE, OF (1974–1989)

His astonishing numbers during his three-year peak from 1977 to 1979—.320/.376/.572, 200-plus hits, three total bases titles, three top-five MVP finishes—were aided by a hitter-friendly Fenway Park, but even adjusting for that, he was 55 percent better than the average hitter. His 383 homers and 1,451 RBI are fourth in team history after Yaz, Williams, and Big Papi.

DAVID ORTIZ, DH (2003–2016)

Signed as a free agent after Minnesota released him rather than raise his pay via arbitration, Big Papi's place in Red Sox lore would have been established simply by way of his back-to-back extra-inning walk-off hits in the 2004 ALCS, but his 483 home runs are the second-most in Red Sox history and by far the most ever by a DH. In his last season, at age 40, he led the league in doubles, RBI, slugging and OPS. He hit .290/.386/.570 in 14 campaigns and was also a great personality whose face still grins out of billboards throughout New England.

PITCHERS

CY YOUNG, RHP (1901–1908)

The guy whose name is on the award pitched only eight years the Boston Americans, and he was already 34 when he arrived or he'd have ranked higher. He led the brand-new American League in wins in each of its first three seasons, with 33, 32, and 28. He led the league in starts, innings, wins, complete games, and park-adjusted ERA while with the team. He walked 2.9 percent of the batters he faced; no other pitcher walked fewer than 4.2 percent. He and Clemens are tied for the franchise record with 192 wins. In 1906, at 38, he lost 21 and was hit pretty hard by the standards of the day, but the great command was still there and he came roaring back for two more great seasons before being dealt back to Cleveland, where he had begun his career.

SMOKY JOE WOOD, RHP (1908–1915)

Wood had, effectively, two careers, first with Boston as a pitcher and, after his arm gave out, with Cleveland as a right fielder. His 1912 season, when he went 34-5 with a 1.91 ERA and a league-leading 35 complete games (with a record-tying 16 consecutive victories), is one of the best in history. In the fall, he went 3-1 in the World Series, winning the clinching eighth game (there was a tie) over the Giants. Between the regular season and postseason he threw 366 innings; he was never able to pitch even 200 innings again. The tank wasn't completely empty, though: In his last year with Boston, he went 15-5 with a league-leading 1.49 ERA.

DUTCH LEONARD, LHP (1913–1918)

Possessing an intimidating fastball that helped him throw no-hitters in 1916 and 1918, Leonard set an unbreakable record in 1914: 24 earned runs allowed in 224 2/3 innings, a microscopic 0.96 ERA. He compiled a 90-64 record and 2.13 ERA in his time in Boston, finishing in the top ten in the league strikeouts four times and strikeout rate five times. He was a perfect 2-0 with a 1.00 ERA in Boston's World Series wins in 1915 and 1916. He's primarily remembered today for accusing Ty Cobb and Tris Speaker of participating in a game-fixing scheme.

LEFTY GROVE, LHP (1934–1942)

Like Cy Young, Grove is one of the greatest pitchers of all time who joined Boston late in his career. He was 34 when he joined the club via a fire sale trade from the cash-starved Philadelphia A's. After a rocky initial season, after which he had to reinvent himself to account for a reduction of his stuff (which to that point had been historically good), he led the league in ERA and strikeouts in four of the next five years, going 83-41 with a 2.83 ERA. He earned his 300th and last victory in a Boston uniform. The minor league Baltimore Orioles had held him for five years—imagine what he might have accomplished if he'd made the majors before he was 25.

ELLIS KINDER, RHP (1948–1955)

Yet another late-in-life addition to the team, "Old Folks" was 33 when he joined the club in 1948; economic necessity had kept him on the farm instead of playing baseball until well into his 20s, and he didn't get his first call-up until he was 31. A couple of seasons later the hapless Browns traded him to Boston for a few bodies and more than a little of Tom Yakwey's cash. The next season he went 23-6 and led the league with six shutouts. After another year in the rotation, he switched primarily to the bullpen in 1951 and was the league's best reliever for five years. Saves didn't become an official statistic until 1969, but retroactively, Kinder had 80 of them during that stretch, 35 more than anyone else in the league, to go with a 2.67 ERA.

LUIS TIANT, RHP (1971–1978)

A Swiss Army Knife of a pitcher with a wide variety and pitchers and deliveries, Tiant is best remembered for his heroics in the 1975 postseason (3-0 record in four starts, 2.65 ERA). He came to Boston at 30 after the Twins and Braves both released him in the spring of 1971. After an ineffective inaugural season, he started 1972 in the bullpen, was promoted to the rotation, and wound up leading the American League with a 1.91 ERA. For the rest of his Boston career, he started at lest 30 games per year, winning 20 or more games three times. The pitcher who was let go twice before signing with Boston is fifth in team history for starts and wins.

ROGER CLEMENS, RHP (1984–1996)

Yes, his reputation's tarnished, and he left Boston after four seasons in which he went 110-110 with a 3.77 ERA. But the W-L record was a product of bad run support and the ERA was third-best in the league among pitchers with at least 100 starts. From 1986 to 1992 he won three Cy Young Awards and led the league in ERA four times and shutouts five times. His 2,590 strikeouts are by far the most in franchise history. While untangling the good from the bad of Clemens is more a job for philosophers than historians, there is no denying the reality of the things he accomplished in Boston.

TIM WAKEFIELD, RHP (1995–2011)

Like many knuckeballers, Wakefield's career started late (the Red Sox signed him, at 28, after he'd been released by the Pirates) and ended late as well (he was 45 when he threw his last innings for the club). He started 430 games, the most in team history, and relieved 160 more. He's the only pitcher to throw over 3,000 innings for the club, and his 186 wins rank third. (Being a knuckleballer, he also holds the team records for hit batters and wild pitchers, by a lot.) He was 16-8 with a 2.95 ERA as a starter in 1995, led the team with 15 saves four years later, and was back in the rotation, tied for the team lead in starts four years after that.

PEDRO MARTÍNEZ, RHP (1998–2004)

His 1999 to 2003 peak, when he won two Cy Yong Awards and led the league in strikeout, strikeout rate, and ERA four times, is arguably the most dominant five years of pitching in major league history. A slim hurler under six feet tall, facing chemically-enhanced sluggers and playing in the toughest division in baseball, his 2.10 ERA was less than half the league average. Martinez retains the best adjusted ERA (90 percent better than average), strikeout ratio (31 percent of batters faced), and strikeout/walk ratio (5.4) in team history. His acquisition from a strapped Montreal team was the late-20th century equivalent of Tom Yakwey benefitting from Connie Mack's Depression-induced straits to acquire Jimmie Foxx and Lefty Grove, among others.

JON LESTER, LHP (2006–2014)

The remarkably durable lefty joined the Red Sox rotation in September 2007 and other than a couple of missed starts in 2011 due to a lat strain, he didn't miss a start over the remainder of his time in Boston. His 241 starts rank fourth all-time after Wakefield, Clemens, and Young. He gave up one run in three World Series starts (0.43 ERA) in the team's 2007 and 2013 championships. His 3.64 ERA was 20 percent better than the league average.

A Taxonomy of 2020 Abnormalities

by Rob Mains

I'm going to start this with a trivia question. Trust me, it's relevant. Don't bother skipping to the end of the article to find the answer, it's not there.

Only five players have appeared in 140 or more games for 16 straight seasons. Who are they?

It's a trivia question starting off an essay, so you know how this works: Whatever you guessed, you're wrong. It's okay. As someone who purchased this book, chances are good that you're an educated baseball fan. But the circumstances behind 2020 force us to abandon, or at least seriously question, some of our favorite patterns and crutches for evaluating the game we love.

We just completed what was undoubtedly the strangest season in MLB history. No fans, geographically limited schedule, universal DH, seven-inning twin bills, runners on second in extra innings, a 16-team postseason, a club playing at a Triple-A stadium. Some of these changes will likely persist (sorry), but we've never had so many tweaks dumped on us all at once, at least not since they figured out how many balls were in a walk.

And the biggest, of course, was the 60-game season. The 19th century was dotted with teams that went bankrupt before the season ended, but the lone season with only 60 scheduled games was 1877. That year there were only six teams, the league rostered a total of 77 players (just 16 more than the 2020 Marlins), and batters called for pitches to be thrown high or low by the pitcher, who was 50 feet away. We can say the 2020 season was easily the shortest ever for recognizable baseball.

As such, it'll stand out. Few abbreviated seasons do. Just about everybody reading this knows the 1994 season ended after Seattle's Randy Johnson struck out Oakland's Ernie Young for the last out of the Mariners-A's game on August 11. The ensuing player strike wiped out the rest of the season and the postseason. Teams played only 112-117 games that year.

And many of you know that a strike in the middle of the 1981 season split the season in two, resulting in the only Division Series until 1995. Teams played only 103-111 games that year, the shortest regular season since 1885.

Those two seasons are memorable. So when we see that nobody drove in 100 runs in 1981, or that Greg Maddux was the only pitcher with 180 or more innings pitched in 1994, we think, "Of course. Strike year."

But we don't remember other short years. You might not recall that the 1994 strike spilled into the next year, chopping 18 games off the 1995 schedule. You might've read that the 1918 season, played during the last pandemic, ended after Labor Day due to the government's World War I "work or fight" order. A strike erased the first week and a half of the 1972 season, but that year's best known as the last time pitchers batted in the American League.

The point is, while we don't remember small changes to the schedule, we remember the big ones. The 1981 mid-season strike. The 1994 season- and Series-ending strike. And, of course, the pandemic-shortened 2020 season. We won't need a reminder why Marcell Ozuna's 18 homers were the fewest to lead the National League in a century. (Literally; Cy Williams led with 15 in 1920.)

Now, about that trivia question. The five players are Hank Aaron, Brooks Robinson, Pete Rose, Ichiro Suzuki, and Johnny Damon. The one nobody gets, of course, is Damon, and a lot of people miss Ichiro, whose last season of 140-plus games came garbed in the red-orange and ocean blue of Miami when he was 42. That's half of what makes it a good question. The other half is the two guys whom many think made the list but didn't. Lou Gehrig? His streak started in the Yankees' 42nd game of the 1925 season and lasted only 13 seasons after that. And everybody assumes Cal Ripken Jr. did it, having played 2,632 straight games over 17 seasons. But one of those 17 seasons was 1994, when the Orioles played only 112 games.

My point? *I just told you* everybody remembers the 1994 strike year, but everybody forgets it fell in the middle of Ripken's streak, separating the first twelve years from the last four. Just because we recall something doesn't mean it's always at the front of our minds.

Nobody is going to forget 2020, and baseball is obviously not the main reason. But there will come a time in the future when you're looking at a player's or a team's record, and there will be baffling numbers there for 2020, and you'll think, "I wonder what happened." (Not to mention the missing line for minor league players.) Just like you forgot that the 1994 strike limited Ripken to 112 games.

Try not to forget it, though. The 2020 season resulted in weird statistical results for several reasons.

There were only 60 games.
I know, duh. But that had impacts beyond counting stats like Ozuna's home run total or Yu Darvish and Shane Bieber leading the majors with eight wins. (I know, pitcher wins, but still.)

The 162-game season is the longest among major North American sports, and that duration gives us a gift. Over the course of a long season, small variations tend to even out. A player who has a ten-game hot streak will probably have a ten-game cold streak. A team that starts the year losing a bunch of close games will probably win a bunch of them. We get regression to the mean. Statistics stabilize.

Consider flipping a coin. Over the long run, we expect it to come up heads about half the time. But the fewer flips, the more variation there'll be. If you flip a coin six times, probability theory tells us you'll get at least two-third heads about 34 percent of the time. Flip it 30 times, your chance of two-thirds heads drops to five percent.

Or, relevant to this case, if you flip a coin 60 times, your chance of getting at least 36 heads—that's 60 percent—is 7.75 percent. Expand the coin-flipping to 162 times, and the chance of getting 60 percent heads drops to 0.73 percent.

In other words, the odds of an outcome that's 20 percent better (or worse) than expected is *more than ten times higher* when you flip your coin 60 times than when you do it 162 times. Call it small sample size, call lack of mean reversion, or call it luck not evening out, 162 is a lot more predictive than 60. You get much more variation over 60 games than over 162. Bieber's 1.63 ERA and 0.87 FIP aren't something we'd see over a full season, and neither is Javier Baéz's .203/.238/.360.

Some players' lines in 2020 look normal. Brian Anderson had an .811 OPS in 2019 and an .810 OPS in 2020. (He probably would have gotten that last point if he'd been given enough time.) But there are many like Bieber and Baéz, some of them from young players still establishing their talent levels. The answer to the question, "What went right or wrong for that guy in 2020?" is most likely "Nothing, it was just a 2020 thing."

Preseason training was abbreviated for hitters.

Every year, spring training drags. Players get tired of it, fans get tired of it, and you sure can tell sportswriters get tired of it. Yes, something to get everyone into shape is necessary, but does it really have to drag on for over a month? Can't we shorten it?

The 2020 season answered in the negative, at least for hitters. Warren Spahn is credited with saying that hitting is timing and pitching is upsetting timing. It appears nobody had his timing down after the abbreviated July summer camp. Through August 9—18 games into the season—MLB batters were hitting .230/.311/.395 with a .275 BABIP. That BABIP, had it held, would have been the lowest since 1968, the Year of the Pitcher. In recent years it's hovered around .300.

It didn't hold. Play returned to more normal levels the rest of the year: .249/.325/.425 with a .297 BABIP starting August 10. But batters whose play concentrated in those first two weeks wound up with ugly lines. Andrew

Benintendi went on the injured list with a season-ending rib cage strain on August 11. His final line: .103/.314/.128 in 14 games. Franchy Cordero went on the IL with a hamate bone fracture on August 9 and a .154/.185/.231 line. Even though he came back strong in a late September return, it was too late to repair his full-season numbers.

Preseason training was abbreviated for pitchers.

Every year, spring training drags. Players get tired of it, fans get tired of it … wait, I already said that. But the abbreviated preseason was tough on pitchers, too. As noted, they had the upper hand coming out of the gate. But then they lost that hand. And then their arms, too.

The 2020 season was spread over 67 days. During those 67 days, 237 pitchers hit the Injured List, compared to 135 in the first 67 days of 2019. A lot of those IL stints, though, were COVID-19-related. Still, over the first 67 days of the 2019 season, there were 72 pitchers on the IL with arm injuries. That figure jumped to 110 in 2020, a 53 percent increase.

There are a number of factors contributing to pitcher arm injuries, ranging from usage to velocity, but it appears that attenuated preseason training played a role. A lot of pitchers had super-short seasons due to arm woes. Corey Kluber, Roberto Osuna, and Shohei Ohtani combined for seven innings, none after August 8. All suffered arm injuries. We'll never know whether they'd have fared better with a longer preseason, but we can guess how they probably feel.

Everybody played.

Rosters were set to expand from 25 to 26 in 2020, so even if we'd had a normal season, we'd have likely seen 2019's record of 1,410 players on MLB rosters broken. But due to the pandemic, rosters started the year at 30 and were cut to only 28. Add multiple COVID-19 absences and the revolving door caused by poor starts by hitters and a rash of pitcher arm injuries, and 1,289 players appeared in MLB games in 2020. The comparable figure over the first 67 days of the 2019 season was 1,109. That 16 percent increase works out to an average of six more players per team in 2020 compared to a similar slice of 2019. A future look back at 2020 rosters will include a lot of unfamiliar names.

Plus became a minus.

In advanced metrics, we adjust batter and pitcher performance for park and league/era variations. A plus sign appended to the end of a measure means that it's adjusted for park and league. It's scaled to an average of 100, with higher figures above average and lower figures below average. (Similarly, a metric with a minus is also park- and league-adjusted and scaled to 100, with lower values better.) Here at BP, our advanced measure of offensive performance is DRC+. Baseball-Reference has OPS+ and FanGraphs has wRC+.

Using park and league adjustments, we can compare Dante Bichette's 1995 Steroid Era season at pre-humidor Coors Field (.340/.364/.620, 40 homers, 128 RBI, MVP runner-up) with Jim Wynn's 1968 Year of the Pitcher season at the cavernous Astrodome (.269/.376/.474, 26 homers, 67 RBI, no MVP votes). It's not close. DRC+, OPS+, and wRC+ all give the nod to Wynn, handily. This is a useful tool. As my Baseball Prospectus colleague Patrick Dubuque tweeted last fall, "Please note that when I ask how you are, I am already adjusting for era."

The 2020 season messes up plus (and minus) stats for two reasons. First, the park adjustment was based on only 30 home games instead of the usual 81. Everything noted above regarding the short season applies, literally doubly, to park effect calculations. DRC+ uses a single-season park factor. OPS+ uses a three-year average and wRC+ five years. The figure for 2020 is suspect.

Second, OPS+ and wRC+ adjust for league: American and National. (DRC+ adjusts for opponent, regardless of league.) While there were two leagues in 2020, they were an artificial construct. To reduce travel, teams played opponents geographically, not based on league. There weren't two leagues, American and National. There were three, Western, Central, and Eastern.

That makes a difference because teams in the same league played in different run-scoring environments. AL teams scored 4.58 runs per game, NL teams 4.71. That's a small difference. But teams in the East scored 0.21 more runs per game (4.95) than teams in the West (4.74), and they both scored a lot more than Central teams (4.25). Adjusting for league misses that difference, so this book will be safe in that regard, but other sources may be distorted somewhat.

Not every game was a "game."
In 2020, the rising tide of strikeouts was finally stemmed. Strikeouts per team per game fell from 8.8 in 2019 to 8.7 in 2020. That marked the first decline after 14 straight annual increases.

In 2020, the rising tide of strikeouts rose higher. Batters struck out in 23.4 percent of plate appearances compared to 23.0 percent in 2019. That marked the 15th straight annual increase.

Both are true statements.

Because of two rule changes—seven-inning doubleheaders and runners on second in extra innings—games in 2020 were unprecedented in their brevity. There were 37.0 plate appearances per game in 2020. The only years with fewer were 1904 and 1906-1909. The average game in 2020 entailed 8.61 innings pitched, the fewest since 1899.

So when you see any per-game stats for 2020, you need to increase them by 3 or 4 percent to get them on equal footing with recent years.

Boston Red Sox 2021

Or, better, just ignore them. Last year happened. There were major league games contested between major league teams. But when you're looking at those physical or electronic baseball cards, when you're weaving narratives over why this young player's inevitable rise to stardom fell apart or why that old veteran rekindled his magic, don't linger on the 2020 line. It was just too weird.

Thanks to Lucas Apostoleris for research assistance.

—*Rob Mains is an author of Baseball Prospectus.*

Tranches of WAR

by Russell A. Carleton

We ask "replacement level" to be a lot of things. Sometimes contradictory things. Sometimes I wonder if we know what it even means anymore. The original idea was that it represented the level of production that a team could expect to get from "freely available talent", including bench players, minor leaguers, and waiver wire pickups. It created a common benchmark to compare everyone to, and for that reason, it represented an advancement well beyond what was available at the time. In fact, it created a language and a framework for evaluating players that was not just better but *entirely* different than what came before it.

But then we started mumbling in that language. The idea behind "wins above replacement" was one part sci-fi episode and one part mathematical exercise. Imagine that a player had disappeared before the season and suddenly, in an alternate timeline, his team would have had to replace him. The distance between him and that replacement line was his value. We need to talk about that alternate timeline.

Without getting too into 2:00 am "deep conversations" with extensive navel-gazing, it's worth thinking about why one player might not be playing, while another might.

- A player might not be playing because he has a short-term injury or his manager believes that he needs a day off.
- A player might not be playing because he has a longer-term injury that requires him to be on the injured list.

There's a difference here between these two situations. In particular, the first one generally *doesn't* involve a compensatory roster move, while the second one does. It's possible, though not guaranteed, that the person who will be replacing the injured/resting player would be the same in either case. That matters. Teams generally carry a spare part for all eight position players on the diamond, although in the era of a four-player bench, those spare parts usually are the backup plan for more than one spot.

A couple of years ago, I posed a hypothetical question. Suppose that a team had two players in its system fighting for a fourth outfielder spot. One of them was a league average hitter, but would be worth 20 runs below average if allowed to play center field for a full season. One of them was a perfectly average fielder, but would be 15 runs below average as a hitter, if allowed to play an entire season. Which of the two should the team roster? It's tempting to say the second one, as overall, he is the better player. That misses the point. A league average hitter on the bench isn't just a potential replacement for an injured outfielder. He might also pinch hit for the light-hitting shortstop in a key spot. You keep the average hitter on the roster, even though he isn't a hand-in-glove fit for one specific place on the field, because being a bench player is a different job description than being a long-term fill-in for someone. If you find yourself in need of a longer-term fill-in, you can bring the other guy up from AAA.

When we're determining the value of an everyday player though, if he had disappeared before the season and a team would have had to replace his production, they likely would have done it with a player who was a long-term fill-in type because they would have had to replace a guy who played everyday. Maybe that's the same guy that they would have rostered on their bench anyway, but we don't know. It gets to the query of what we hope to accomplish with WAR. Are we looking for an accurate modeling of reality or are we looking for a common baseline to compare everyone to? Both have their uses, but they are somewhat different questions.

Let's talk about another dichotomy.

- A player might not be playing because he isn't very good and is a bench-level player.
- A player might not be playing because there is another player on the team who has a situational advantage that makes him the better choice today. The classic case of this is a handedness platoon. On another day, he might be a better choice.

When we think about player usage, I think we're still stuck in the model that there are starters and there are scrubs. We have plenty of words for bench players or reserves or backups or utility guys. We do still have the word "platoon" in our collective vocabulary, but in the age of short benches, it's hard to construct one. It's always been hard to construct them. You have to find two players who hit with different hands, have skill sets that complement each other, and probably play the same position. In the era of the short bench, one of them had probably better double as a utility player in some way. Baseball has a two-tiered language geared toward the idea of regulars and reserves. The fact that it was so easy for me to find plenty of synonyms for "a player whose primary function is to come into a game to replace a regular player if he is injured or resting" should tell you something.

I'm always one to look for "unspoken words" in baseball. What is it called when someone is both half of a platoon and the utility infielder? That guy exists sometimes, but he reveals himself in that role—usually by accident. We don't have a word for that, and whenever I find myself saying "we don't have a word for that", I look for new opportunities. What do you call it, further, when the job of being the utility infielder is decentralized across the whole infield with occasional contributions from the left fielder? It's not even a "super-utility" player. What happens when you build your entire roster around the idea that everyone will be expected to be a triple major?

⚾   ⚾   ⚾

I think someone else beat me to this one, and on a grand scale. Platoons work because we know that hitters of the opposite hand to the pitcher get better results than hitters of the same hand, usually to the tune of about 20 points of OBP. If you want to express that in runs, it usually comes out to somewhere around 10 to 12 runs of linear weights value prorated across 650 PA. But hang on a second, now let's say that we have two players who might start today, both of roughly equal merit with the bat. One has a handedness advantage, but is the worse fielder of the two. In that case, as long as his "over the course of a season" projection as a fielder at whatever position you want to slot him into is less than a 10-run drop from the guy he might replace, then he's a better option today.

We're not used to thinking of utility players as bat-first options, who would play below-average defense at three different infield positions. That guy might hook on as a 2B/3B/LF type (Howie Kendrick, come on down!) but teams usually think to themselves that they need as their utility infielder someone who "can handle" shortstop, the toughest of the infield spots to play. If someone can do that *and* hit well, he's probably already starting somewhere, so he's not available as a utility infielder. It's easier for those glove guys to find a job. In a world where the replacement for a shortstop *has to be* the designated utility infielder, that makes sense.

But as we talked about last week, we're living in a different world. The rate at which a replacement for a regular starter turns out to be *another starter* shifting over to cover has gone way up over the last five years. There was always some of it in the game, but this has been a supernova of switcheroos. Now if your second baseman is capable of playing a decent shortstop, that 2B/3B/LF guy can swap in. He's not actually playing shortstop, and maybe the defense suffers from the switch, but if he's got enough of a bat, he might outhit those extra fielding miscues. And in doing so, he is effectively your backup shortstop.

Somewhere along the lines, teams got hip to the idea of multi-positional play from their regulars. I've written before about how you can't just put a player, however athletic, into a new position and expect much at first. The data tell us that. Eventually, players can learn to be multi-positionalists, but it takes time, roughly on the order of two months, before they're OK. But there's a hidden message in there. If you give a player some reps at a new spot, he's a reasonably gifted athlete and somewhat smart and willing to learn, he could probably pick it up enough to get to "good enough," and it doesn't take forever. You just have to be purposeful about it. Maybe you get to the point where you can start to say "he's still below average but we could move him there and get another bat into the lineup, and it's a net win."

Teams have started to build those extra lessons into their player development program. It used to be seen as a mark of weakness to be relegated to "utility player" because that meant that you were a bench player (all those synonyms above come with a side of stigma). Now, it's a way of building a team. If you get a few reps in the minors (where it doesn't count) at a spot, you'll have at least played the spot at game speed before. There are limits to how far you can push that. A slow-footed "he's out in left field because we don't have the DH" guy is never going to play short, but maybe your third baseman can try second base and not look like a total moose out there.

⚾ ⚾ ⚾

Back to WAR. I'd argue that the world of starters and scrubs is slowly disintegrating, for good cause. In the event that a regular starter really does go down with an injury–ostensibly, the alternate universe scenario that WAR is attempting to model–it makes the team a little more resilient to replacing him. And the good news is that you're more likely to be able to replace him with the best of the bench bunch, rather than the third-best guy, because the best guy doesn't have to be an exact positional match for the guy who got hurt. And that's what the manager would want to do. He'd want to replace that long-term production, not with an amalgam of everyone else who played that position, but with the best guy available from his reserves.

Now this is still WAR. We still want to retain the principle that we should be measuring a player, and not his teammates. We need some sort of common baseline, and despite what I just said, we'll still need some sort of amalgam. To construct that, I give to you the idea of the tranche. The word, if you've not heard it before, refers to a piece of a whole that is somehow segmented off. It's often used in finance to talk about layers of a financial instrument.

Here, I want you to consider that there are 30 starters at each of the seven non-battery positions (catchers should have their own WAR, since only a catcher can replace a catcher). We can identify them by playing time, and we can futz around with the definition a little bit if we need to. Next, among those who aren't in that starting pool, we identify the top tranche of the 30 best bench players, which I would again identify by playing time, and then the second and third and fourth and so on. If a player were to disappear, his manager would probably want to take a guy from that top tranche of the bench to replace him. In a world where even the starters can slide around the field, that becomes more feasible.

We can take a look at that top tranche and say "How many of them showed that they are able to play (first, second, etc.)?" and therefore could have directly substituted for the starter? How many of them could have been a direct substitute for our injured player? We don't know whether one of them would be on *a specific* team, but we can say that 40 percent of the time, a manager would have been able to draw from tranche 1 in filling the role, and 35 percent from tranche 2. But on tranche 1, we can also look at how many of those players played a position that could have then shifted and covered for that spot. We'd need some eligibility criteria for all of this (probably a minimum number of games played) but it would just be a matter of multiplication. Shortstop would be harder to fill, and managers would probably be dipping a little further down in the talent pool, and so replacement level would be lower, as it is now.

Doing some quick analysis, I found that the difference in just batting linear weights (haven't even gotten into running or fielding) between tranche 1 and tranche 2 in 2019 was about 6.5 runs, prorated across 650 PA. Between tranche 1 and tranche 3, it's 10.8 runs. The ability to shift those plate appearances up the ladder has some real value.

This part is important. We can also give credit to starters for the positions that they showed an ability to play, even if they didn't play them (this is the guy fully capable of playing center, but who's in a corner because the team already has a good center fielder) because he allows a team to carry a player who hits like a left fielder to functionally be the team's backup center fielder. He facilitates that movement upward among the tranches. We can start to appreciate the difference between a left fielder who would never be able to hack it in center (and the compensatory move that his team would have to make) and the left fielder who could do it, but just didn't have to very often.

Past that, you can continue to use whatever hitting and fielding and running metrics you like to determine a player's value, but when we get down to constructing that baseline, I'd argue we need a better conceptual and mathematical framework. It's going to require some more #GoryMath than we're used to, but I'd argue it's a better conceptualization of the way that MLB actually plays the game in 2020. If…y'know…MLB plays in 2020. If WAR is going to be our flagship statistic among the *acronymati*, then we need to acknowledge that it contains some old and starting-to-be-out-of-date assumptions about the game. We may need to tinker with it. Here's my idea for how.

—*Russell A. Carleton is an author of Baseball Prospectus.*

Secondhand Sport

by Patrick Dubuque

Back before time stopped, I liked to go to thrift stores. Now that I'm older, I rarely ever buy anything—I don't need much in my life, now—but I still enjoy the old familiar circuit: check to see if there are baseball cards to write about, look for board or card games to play with the kids, scan for random ironic jerseys, hit the book section. It takes ten, maybe fifteen minutes. Thrift stores are the antithesis of modern online shopping, because you don't know what they have, and you don't even really know what you want. It's junk, literal junk, stuff other people thought was worthless. That's what makes it great.

In an idealized economy, thrift stores shouldn't exist. Everybody has a living wage, and every product has a durability that exactly matches its desired life; nothing should need to be given away, no one should need to be given to. But then, thrift stores shouldn't work on a customer experience level, either. You wouldn't think an ethos of "let's make everything disorganized and hard to find" would lead to customer satisfaction, but low-budget retailers like TJ Maxx and Ross thrive on this model. People like bargain hunting as much for the hunting as the bargain; it's part of the experience, spending time as if it's a wager. There's a thrill, occasionally, in inefficiency.

In sports, the modern overuse of the word "inefficiency" is a condemnation: It insinuates that there is *an* efficiency, a correct way to be found, and that all other ways are wrong ways. It's prevalent in baseball but hardly contained to it; the lifehack, the Silicon Valley disruption are other examples of productivity creep in our daily lives. Their modern success makes plenty of sense. Maximization of resources, after all, is its own puzzle, and an industry of European board games is founded upon it. It's fun to take a system and optimize it, unravel it like a sudoku puzzle. If there's only one kind of genius, after all, there's no way anyone can fail to appreciate it.

Baseball has been hacking away at these perceived inefficiencies since its inception: platoons, bullpens, farm systems were all installed to extract more out of the tools at hand. But it's been a particular badge of the sabermetric movement, from Ken Phelps and his All-Star Team to Ricardo Rincon and the darlings of *Moneyball*. It's business, but it's also an ethos: the idea that there's treasure among the trash, something we all failed to appreciate until someone brought it to light.

It's the myth that made Sidd Finch so enticing, that fuels so many "best shape" narratives and new pitch promises. We all, athletes and unathletic sportswriters, want to believe that there's genius trapped inside us, and that it's just a matter of puzzling out the combination to unlock it. That our art, our style is the next inefficiency, waiting for our own Billy Beane. It's why we root for underdogs, and why we're excited for the Mike Tauchmans and the Eurubiel Durazos, champions of skin-deep mediocrity.

Except we aren't anymore, really. The days of "Free X" have descended beyond the ring of irony and into obscurity. There are still Xs to be freed, or at least one X, duplicated endlessly: Mike Ford, Luke Voit, Max Muncy. The undervalued one-dimensional slugger demonstrated how the game hasn't quite culturally caught up to its logical extreme. But for those who don't fit the rather spacious mold, times are grimmer. As Rob Arthur revealed several months ago, there's been a marked increase in the number of sub-replacement relievers. It's the outcome of a greater number of teams forced to play out games without the talent to win them, but it's also emblematic of the modern tendency of teams to dispose of their disposable assets, burning through cost-controlled arms the way that man chopped down forests in *The Lorax*. Stuff just isn't built to outlive their original owners anymore.

It's unsurprising, given how well-mined the market for inefficiencies has been of late. The disciples of the early analytics departments, and the disciples of those, have proliferated the league, with only a few backwater holdouts. The league has grown smarter, but every team has learned the same lesson. In fact, the phenomenon creates a peculiar kind of feedback loop: As teams value a specific subset of players or skills, prospective athletes learn to increase their own marketability by conforming themselves to the demands of their prospective employers.

And that's tragic, in the way that the extinction of animals is tragic; a certain amount of biodiversity in baseball has been lost. Shortstops hit like outfielders. Pitchers don't hit at all. Only the catchers remain idiosyncratic, thanks to the defensive demands of their position; eventually they too will be required to produce like everyone else, or they'll meet the fate of their battery mates. A perfect economy requires perfect production.

I mentioned earlier that more and more, I leave thrift stores empty-handed. It is true that I am more discerning than in the past; my bookshelves are full, and there are more streaming films than I will ever be able to watch. But there are other factors at play.

Thrift stores are, in a way, the bond markets of retail. When the economy is rough and other retailers are struggling, more people look secondhand for their products. But as recently as last year, publications were noting a reversal of the trend: Companies like Goodwill and Savers were expanding despite a strong economy. Publications credited a heightened sense of environmentalism and a rejection of cutting-edge fashion as drivers behind the increase, though the more likely answer is the modern American economy hasn't showered its favors equally, particularly among the young.

But it is more than just the economy. Baseball and thrift stores share something else in common, evident in our current conversations about re-starting the sport: They live in the gray area between public service and private enterprise. Thrift stores provide affordable necessities to lower-class citizens, and collectibles and fashion for the middle-class. Because of the success of the latter, prices have gone up across the board. Especially in terms of clothing, the middle-class flight from fashion into vintage has instead carried the aftereffects of fashion, including its costs, into a territory where people just want clothes. But there's another factor in the rise of prices, in the form of the internet.

The Goodwills of the world have grown smarter, too, employing the internet to extract full value from their detritus. Ebay, similarly, has lost much of the charm it had as a new frontier around the turn of the century. Everything has a price point now; even individual taste is no match for the algorithm, because anything rare, no matter how niche its market, is a collectible to someone.

The internet has had the same effect on thrift stores that sabermetrics has had on baseball; its equivalent to OBP was the bar scanner. As detailed in Slate, the rise of second-party stores on eBay and Amazon birthed an entire industry of used-good salespeople, armed with PDAs and scanners, buying books for three dollars to sell online for five. The author, Michael Savitz, reports earning $60,000 by working nearly 80 hours a week; he makes it clear that this is not a vocation of his choosing. It's long hours, with no real creativity or individuality, skimming the cream off of a local establishment and flipping it to someone with a little more money on the other side of the country. And once the vocation exists, the obvious question arises: why wait to put the wares out on the shelves? Why allow value to exist at all?

Nothing is ruined. Thrift stores will continue to sell polo shirts and DVDs, and baseball will continue to exist and make or lose money, depending on who you believe. But as we continue to refine our knowledge, we lose something in the conquest for efficiency, a delight born out of the unknown. The problem isn't the efficiency itself; we can't blame the booksellers, or the people sweeping freeways to collect grams of platinum from damaged catalytic converters. The problem is a system that requires this sort of profit-skimming behavior in order to feed families (or, for corporations, maximize shareholder return).

In times like these, with the 2020 season on the brink and the collective bargaining agreement close behind, it can often feel like the current situation is untenable. It can't keep going like this, even if we don't know what to do about it. But as with thrift stores, there's an equally irresistible feeling that it *has* to keep going, that it would be unimaginable to not have this broken, amazing sport. Both industries exist on an invisible foundation of friction, of chaos and unpredictability, even as both see their foundations buffed down to a perfect, untouchable polish. But if COVID-19 and its financial ramifications do, as some have suggested, make it such that the baseball that returns is fundamentally different than the baseball that came before, perhaps this is the time to lean in, and change the game even more. Fix bunting. Make defense more difficult. Create viable, alternate strategies. Add some chaos back into baseball. It's fun when no one knows quite where things are.

—Patrick Dubuque is an author of Baseball Prospectus.

Steve Dalkowski Dreaming

by Steven Goldman

We dream of being a pitcher, of starring in the major leagues. Depending on your age and your sense of historical perspective, you might imagine yourself as Walter Johnson, throwing harder than anyone else—hitting more batters than anyone else, too, but always feeling bad about it. You could picture yourself as a Tom Seaver or a David Cone, with all the stuff in the world but still being cerebral about it, thinking about so much more than burning 'em in there. There are so many models one could choose: You could be a Lefty Gomez, Jim Bouton, or Bill Lee, skilled, but not taking the whole thing too seriously, or a Lefty Grove, Bob Gibson, or Steve Carlton, powerful but treating each start like a mission to be survived instead of a game to be enjoyed.

Very few would dream of being Steve Dalkowski, the former Baltimore Orioles prospect who died of COVID-19 last week at the age of 80. Yet, there is something just as noble in Dalkowski's negative accomplishments—and accomplishments is what they are—as there is in the precision-engineered pitching of a Greg Maddux. You have to be very good to be that bad. Dalkowski had all of the stuff of the greatest pitchers but none of the command; his story is not one of failing to conquer his limitations, but striving against one of the cruelest hands that fate or genetics or personality can deal us: A desire to achieve great things which is almost but not quite matched by the ability to meet that goal.

As with Johnson, Grove, Bob Feller, and the rest of the hard-throwing pitchers who played before the advent of modern radar guns, we have to take the word of the players and coaches who saw Dalkowski pitch as to his velocity. He was a hard-drinking, maximum-effort pitcher who, if their memories are to be believed, consistently threw over 100 miles per hour. His was the Maltese Fastball, the stuff that dreams are made of. The problem is that velocity without command and control is still a good distance from utility. Dalkowski was the most effective towel you could design for a fish, the sleekest bathing suit intended to be worn by an astronaut, but that doesn't mean he wasn't beautiful: We can appreciate a journey even if it doesn't end at the intended destination.

Whether because of sloppy mechanics he couldn't calm, an inability to understand that a consistent 98 in the strike zone would likely be more effective than a consistent 110 out of it, or all that beer, Dalkowski could never make the adjustments that pitchers like Feller and Nolan Ryan made before him, possibly because he had so far to go: Feller, who never pitched in the minors, came up at 17 and spent three years walking almost seven batters per nine innings before settling in at 3.8 beginning when he was 20. Ryan started out walking over six batters per nine but gradually improved as his long career played out; for him to go from 6.2 walks per nine with the 1966 Greenville Mets to 3.7 with the 1989 Texas Rangers represents a 40 percent reduction. An equivalent improvement by Dalkowski would still have left him walking over 11 batters per nine innings.

Dalkowski was like *The Room* of pitchers, a player so bad he became good again. Cal Ripken, Sr., who both played with and managed Dalkowski, recalled in a 1979 *Sporting News* "where are they now" piece the occasion when the pitcher crossed up his catcher and his fastball, "hit the plate umpire smack in the mask. The mask broke all to pieces and the umpire wound up in the hospital for three days with a concussion. If they ever had a radar gun in those days, I'll bet Dalkowski would have been timed at 110 miles an hour."

Signed by the Orioles out of New Britain High in Connecticut in 1957, Dalkowski was sent to Kingsport in the Appalachian League, where he pitched 62 innings. He allowed only 22 hits in 62 innings, or 3.2 per nine, a number with no equivalent in major league history (though Aroldis Chapman came close in 2014), and also struck out 121 (17.6 per nine) and walked 129 (18.7). He was also charged with 39 wild pitches. That June, one of his fastballs clipped a Dodgers prospect named Bob Beavers and carried away part of his ear. "The first pitch was over the backstop, the second pitch was called a strike, I didn't think it was," Beavers said last year. "The third pitch hit me and knocked me out, so I don't remember much after that. I couldn't get in the sun for a while, and I never did play baseball again." Former minor leaguer Ron Shelton based the *Bull Durham* pitcher Nuke LaLoosh on Dalkowski. And yet, to see him as a figure of fun, an amusing loser, is to misunderstand something unique and strange.

Dalkowski kept on posting some of the strangest lines in baseball history. Pitching for the Stockton Ports of the Class C California League in 1960, he struck out 262 and walked 262 in 170 innings. Yet, he did improve, especially after pitching for Earl Weaver at Elmira in 1962. Weaver had previously had Dalkowski at Aberdeen in 1959, but wasn't ready to grapple with him then. This time he was. "I had grown more and more concerned about players with great physical abilities who could not learn to correct certain basic deficiencies no matter how much you instructed or drilled them," he related in his autobiography, *It's What You Learn After You Know It All That Counts*. He got permission from the Orioles to give all of his players the Stanford-Binet IQ test. "Dalkowski finished in the 1 percentile in his ability to understand facts. Steve, it was said to say, had the ability to do everything but learn." [sic]

IQ tests are problematic diagnostic tools, so take Weaver's estimate of Dalkowski's mental capabilities with a grain of salt. What's important is that even if he got to the right answer by way of the wrong reason, Weaver had learned something valuable. His insight was to stop asking Dalkowski to learn new pitches and just let him get by with the two that he had. Were Dalkowski a prospect today, that would have been a no-brainer: Can't develop a third pitch? The bullpen is right over there, sir. Player development wasn't like that then, but Weaver, temporarily Dalkowski's mentor, could let him work with what he had. According to Weaver, the pitcher responded: "In the final 57 innings he pitched that season Dalkowski gave up 1 earned run, struck out 110 batters, and walked only 11." It's not true—as per the *Elmira Star-Gazette*, as of late July, Dalkowski had walked 71 in 106 innings and finished with 114 in 160 innings, which means Dalkowski's control actually faded at the end of the season rather than improved—but that doesn't mean it didn't happen in some sense, just that it didn't happen that way. Again, it's the journey, not the destination, and his ERA was 3.04 so *something* had gone right.

Also along the way: The next spring, Orioles manager Billy Hitchcock was rooting for Dalkowski to make the team as a long-man—maybe Weaver had gotten through to him. There were things out of Weaver's control, like the universe's twisted sense of humor: that March, Dalkowski's elbow went "twang."

You sometimes read that it was the Orioles' insistence on Dalkowski learning the curve that did him in, but even if they hadn't learned their lesson, the injury was probably just a coincidence: Dalkowski had thrown an incredible number of pitches over the previous few years. Still, it testifies to the dangers of trying to get what you want and risking the loss of what you had. Dalkowski tried to come back, but the 110-mph stuff was gone. A pitcher with no control and no stuff is…a civilian. What followed were years of vagabond living, arrests for drunkenness. There were Alcoholics Anonymous meetings, assistance from baseball alumni associations, but none of it took. From the 1990s until the time of his passing he dwelt in an assisted living facility, suffering from alcohol-related dementia. He'd been a heavy drinker since his teenage years. As with all those pitches per game, there was a price to be paid. You make choices on the journey and some of them are irrevocable. It's like a fairy tale: "Bite of poison apple? Don't mind if I do."

In the aforementioned *Sporting News* profile, Chuck Stevens, the head of the Association of Professional Ballplayers of America, a ballplayer charity, said, "I've got nothing against drinking. I do it myself sometimes. But, I don't condone common drunkenness. We went through lots of heartache and many dollars, but Dalkowski didn't want to help himself and we weren't going to keep him drunk." The journey is *un*like a fairy tale: No one will come along and kiss it better, not if they're busy forming judgments.

In the end, we are left with a sort of philosophical chicken/egg conundrum: Is failing to meet your goals evidence of unfulfilled potential or the lack of it? Isn't what you did by definition what you were capable of doing? Or could you have broken through to something better with the right help, the right lucky break? These are unanswerable questions, and how we try to answer them may say more about us than about the people we're judging.

No pitcher ever has it easy. *All* pitchers must work hard. *All* pitchers must refine their craft. It's almost never just about *stuff*. Dalkowski dreaming is no insult to the great pitchers who made it; from Pete Alexander to Max Scherzer, they have all earned their way up. And yet, if it is true that we can only do as much as we can do, then the journey would be more of an adventure, the ultimate triumph or defeat more noble, if like Dalkowski we lacked 100 percent of the confidence, the command, the self-possession, the commitment, the resistance to making bad decisions that so many great players possess—to be gloriously human. Or, to put it more succinctly, it would be fun to be able to throw as hard as any person ever has. Even if just for a moment, and even if nothing more came of it than that, no one could say you hadn't lived life to the fullest.

—*Steven Goldman is an author of Baseball Prospectus.*

A Reward For A Functioning Society

by Cory Frontin and Craig Goldstein

On July 5, Nationals reliever Sean Doolittle said in the middle of a press conference regarding the restart of Major League Baseball and what would later be known as summer camp, "sports are like the reward of a functioning society." This sentence was amidst a much longer, thoughtful reply about the societal and health conditions under which MLB players were being brought back. It's a very similar sentiment to one Jane McManus used on April 7, when she discussed the White House's meeting with sports commissioners. She said "sports are the effect of a functioning society—not the precursor."

Both versions of the same sentiment spoke to a laudable ideal in the context of a country that was not addressing a rampaging virus, and opting instead to bring sports back for the feeling of normalcy rather than the reality of it. "Priorities," as McManus said.

On Wednesday, the NBA's Milwaukee Bucks conducted a wildcat/political strike, refusing to come out for Game 5 of their playoff series against the Orlando Magic. The Magic refused to accept the forfeit, and shortly thereafter other playoff series were threatened by player strikes. Eventually the league moved to postpone that day's games, folding to players leveraging their united power.

The backdrop against which these actions took place was the shooting by police of Jacob Blake. Blake was shot in the back seven times by police, as he attempted to get into his vehicle. He managed to survive the assault, but is paralyzed from the waist down.

⚾ ⚾ ⚾

The step taken to walk out, first by the Milwaukee Bucks, then subsequently by other NBA, WNBA, and MLB teams, was a step toward upholding the virtue of the sentiment described by McManus and Doolittle. But that sentiment does not align with the broad history of sports in this and other countries, a history that contradicts the core of the idealistic statement.

Sports have been a significant part of American society for most of its existence, expanding in importance and influence in recent years. The idea that society was functioning in a way that was worthy of the reward of sports for most of that time is laughable. Much of America is not functioning and has not functioned for Black people, full stop. The oppressed people at the center of this political act by players, specifically Black players, in concert throughout the NBA and in fits and starts throughout Major League Baseball, have not known a society that functions for them rather than *because* of them.

Politics has been part of the sports landscape since the inception of sport, but for just about as long people have bemoaned its presence. Sports are to be an escape, it is said. An escape from what, though? A functioning society?

No, the presence of sports has never signified a cultural or political system that is on the up and up. Rather, the presence of sports *reflect and reinforce the society that produces them*.

⚾ ⚾ ⚾

The Negro Leagues were born out of societal dysfunction. The need for entirely separate leagues, composed of Black and Latino players barred from the Major Leagues because of racism? That is not a functioning society, and yet there were sports.

Even the integration of players from the Negro Leagues resulted in a transfer of power and wealth from Black-owned businesses and communities and into white ones, mirroring the dysfunction that had bled into every aspect of American society at the time. Japheth Knopp noted in the Spring 2016 Baseball Research Journal:

> *The manner in which integration in baseball—and in American businesses generally—occurred was not the only model which was possible. It was likely not even the best approach available, but rather served the needs of those in already privileged positions who were able to control not only the manner in which desegregation occurred, but the public perception of it as well in order to exploit the situation for financial gain. Indeed, the very word integration may not be the most applicable in this context because what actually transpired was not so much the fair and equitable combination of two subcultures into one equal and more homogenous group, but rather the reluctant allowance—under certain preconditions—for African Americans to be assimilated into white society.*

To understand the value of a movement, though, is not to understand how it is co-opted by ownership, but to know the people it brings together and what they demand. When Jackie Robinson—the player who demarcated the inevitability of the end of the Negro leagues—attended the March on Washington for Jobs and Freedom in 1963, he did so with his family and marched alongside the people. He stood alongside hundreds of thousands to fight for their common civil and labor rights. "The moral arc of the universe is long," many freedom fighters have echoed, "but it bends towards justice." The bend, it is less frequently said, happens when a great mass of people place the moral arc of the universe on their knee and apply force, as Jackie, his family, and thousands of others did that day.

⚾ ⚾ ⚾

Of course, taking the moral arc of the universe down from the mantle and bending it is not without risk. Perhaps the outsized influence of athletes is itself a mark of a dysfunctional society, but, nonetheless, hundreds of athletes woke up on Wednesday morning with the power to bring in millions of dollars in revenues. That very power, as we would come to find out, was matched with the equal and opposite power to *not* bring those revenues. That power, in hands ranging from the Milwaukee Bucks, to Kenny Smith in the *Inside the NBA* Studio, from the unexpected ally, Josh Hader, and his largely white teammates to the notably Black Seattle Mariners, would be exercised for a single demand: the end to state violence against Black people. Not unlike the March itself, it sat at the intersection of the civil rights of Black Americans and bold labor action. The March on Washington stood in the face of a false notion of integration—against an integration of extraction but not one of equality—and proposed something different. Just the same, the acts of solidarity of August 26, 2020 will be remembered in stark defiance of MLB's BLM-branded, but ultimately empty displays on opening weekend.

Bold defiance like this can never be without risk. By choosing to exercise this power, the Milwaukee Bucks took a risk. They risked vitriol and backlash from those they disagreed with. They risked fines or seeing their contracts voided, as a walkout like this is prohibited by their CBA. They risked forfeiting a playoff game, one that, as the No. 1 seed in the playoffs, they'd worked all year to attain. They didn't know how Orlando would respond. It wasn't clear that other teams throughout the league would follow suit in solidarity. And it wasn't known the league would accept these actions and moderately co-opt them by "postponing" games that would have featured no players.

If the league reschedules the games, some of the athletes' risk—their shared sacrifice—will be diminished, in retrospect. But they did not know any of that when they took that risk. And it is often left to athletes to take these risks when others in society won't, especially those of their same socioeconomic status and levels of influence.

It is athletes, specifically BIPOC athletes, that take them, though, because they live with the risk of being something other than white in this country every day. They are no strangers to the realities of police brutality. It seems incongruous then, to say that sports are a reward for a functioning society when we rely on athletes to lead us closer to being a functioning society. Luckily, our beloved athletes, WNBA players first and foremost among them, understand what sports truly are: a pipebender for the moral arc of the universe.

—Craig Goldstein is editor in chief of Baseball Prospectus. Cory Frontin is an author of Baseball Prospectus.

Index of Names

Andriese, Matt 44
Araúz, Jonathan 16
Arroyo, Christian 18
Barnes, Matt 46
Blalock, Bradley 111
Bogaerts, Xander 20
Bradley Jr., Jackie 22
Brasier, Ryan 48
Brewer, Colten 50
Brice, Austin 52
Casas, Triston 82, 103
Castillo, Rusney 83
Chavis, Michael 24
Cordero, Franchy 84
Cuevas, William 91
Dalbec, Bobby 26, 107
Devers, Rafael 28
Downs, Jeter 85, 104
Duran, Jarren 85, 105
Eovaldi, Nathan 54
Feltman, Durbin 92
Godley, Zack 56
Groome, Jay 93, 112
Hernandez, Darwinzon 58
Hernández, Enrique 30
Houck, Tanner 60, 109
Jimenez, Gilberto 86, 109
Jordan, Blaze 87, 111
Leyer, Robinson 62
Liu, Chih-Jung 111
Lugo, Matthew 87, 108

Martinez, J.D. 32
Mata, Bryan 94, 106
Mazza, Chris 64
McHugh, Collin 94
Muñoz, Yairo 34
Murphy, Chris 111
Ottavino, Adam 66
Pedroia, Dustin 88
Pérez, Martín 68
Pivetta, Nick 70
Plawecki, Kevin 36
Potts, Hudson 88
Renfroe, Hunter 38
Richards, Garrett 72
Rodriguez, Eduardo 95
Rosario, Jeisson 89
Sale, Chris 96
Sawamura, Hirokazu 97
Seabold, Connor 98, 110
Song, Noah 98, 104
Springs, Jeffrey 74
Taylor, Josh 99
Valdez, Phillips 76
Vázquez, Christian 40
Verdugo, Alex 42
Walden, Marcus 78
Ward, Thad 100, 110
Weber, Ryan 80
Whitlock, Garrett 100
Wong, Connor 89
Wu-Yelland, Jeremy 111

Boston Red Sox 2021

Yorke, Nick 90, 108

For the Joy of Keeping Score

THIRTY81 Project is an ongoing graphic design project focused on the ballparks of baseball. Since being established in 2013, scorecards have been a fundemantal part of the effort. Each two-page card is uniquely ballpark-centric — there are 30 variants — and designed with both beginning and veteran scorekeepers in mind. Evolving over the years with suggestions from fans, broadcasters, and official scorers, the sheets are freely available to everyone as printable letter-size PDFs at the project webshop: www.THIRTY81Project.com

Download, Print, Score, Repeat …

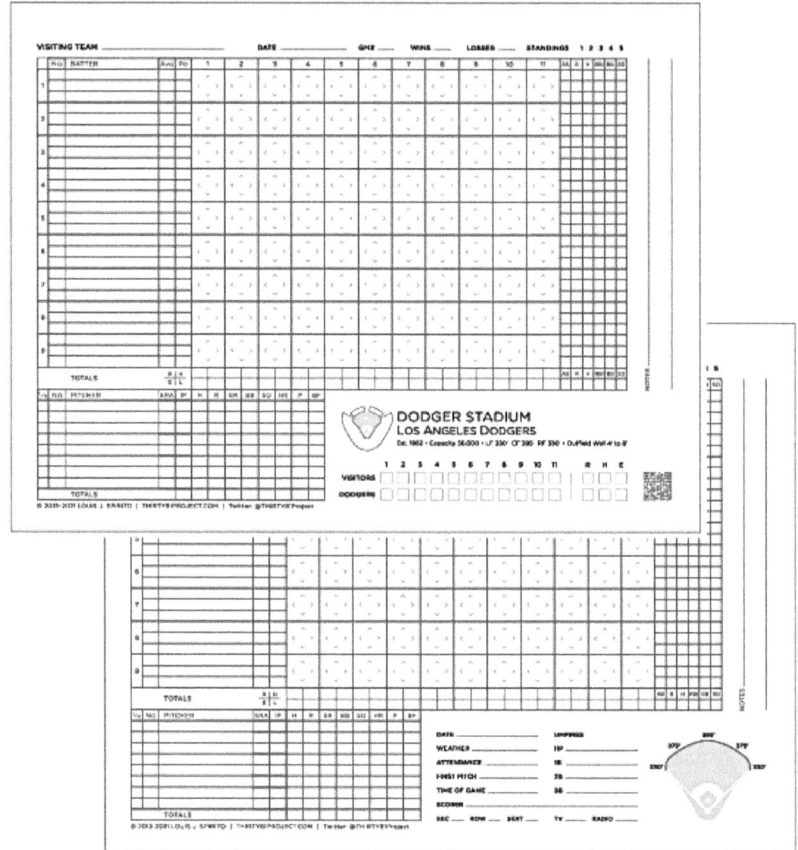

Scorecard design ©2013-2021 Louis J. Spirito | THIRTY81Project